ADVANCE PRAISE FOR
The Overly Honest Teacher

"If you're like me, you were dying to be a fly on the wall in your little kid's classroom, and with this book you get to be. Meredith Essalat, a veteran of the classroom, gives us a brave and tender sneak peek into our children's little world, serving as a much-needed bridge between parents and educators."

—Jill Kargman, writer and star of the television show *Odd Mom Out*, based on her novel *Momzillas*. She is a *New York Times* bestselling author and has written for *Vogue, Elle, Harper's Bazaar, GQ,* and many other magazines as well as television shows.

"The partnership between school and family is tantamount to the overall mental and academic health of our students. Meredith definitely puts it on the table in this book. She is vulnerable, honest, and clear in her messaging. Parents and educators alike would be better served if we took her advice."

—Elaine Barry, Ed.D, Director, Sophie's Scholars Program, Sacred Heart Schools, Atherton, California

"Meredith Essalat offers an inside track to your children's mind and how to empower them to own their own achievements. She lists dos and don'ts on how to communicate with your children. In an age of declining common decency, Meredith also guides us in raising good humans."

—Jennifer Chou Nocerini, co-author of *New York Times* bestseller *The Only Three Questions That Count* and mother of two

"As a single father to ten-year-old twin girls, I have always relied on my 'little village' in helping rear and care for my daughters. Meredith's honesty, passion, integrity, and love for what she does and for our children rings true in every chapter of this book. I am a huge fan of this book and its heartfelt message."

—David Kirsch, wellness visionary and founder of the award-winning Madison Square Club in New York City

"A brilliant combination of emotional guidance and intellect, *The Overly Honest Teacher* diligently examines the lives between parents, children, and scholar. A well-thought-out journey and navigation tool for parents of school-age children, *The Overly Honest Teacher* is a fantastic template that uses knowledge and passion to effectively guide parents through the tender and complicated primary school years."

—Kate Rouchell, President, KGB LLC

"*The Overly Honest Teacher* is a must-read for every parent. It could easily replace a school's handbook! [Meredith Essalat's] guidance to parents is on target. Most importantly, children thrive from an honest, authentic collaboration between parents and teachers. It is a win-win for them."

—...tional consultant and Superintendent of Schools,

PARENTING ADVICE FROM THE CLASSROOM

The OVERLY HONEST TEACHER

By Meredith Essalat, M.Ed.

THE
collective.
BOOK STUDIO

Library of Congress cataloguing-in-publication data available.
ISBN: 978-1-951412-05-0
Ebook ISBN: 978-1-951412-15-9
LCCN: 2020900509

Manufactured in China.
Design by Andrea Kelly.

10 9 8 7 6 5 4 3 2 1

The Collective Book Studio
Oakland, California

To adequately express my gratitude to each individual who has influenced this book would be an insurmountable task. So instead I say, to everyone I have ever known—my family, my friends, my students and their parents, my colleagues— a thousand times I thank you.

CONTENTS

PREFACE

Young people today are under tremendous pressure to live up to high expectations. In order to support our students and guide them to success, we adults must be willing to do as Meredith is doing here—be overly honest.

When I first started teaching, more than thirty years ago, it was by chance, not design. That chance encounter changed not just my career path, but my life's journey. I remember my first day as a teacher's aide, looking at the clock at the end of the day and marveling that it was time for the students to go home. It was the first job I had that the day didn't drag on. I was energized and knew I had found my calling.

Over the years, I've learned that regardless of class, race, socioeconomic status, or education level, most parents and teachers want children to succeed and be the best they can be. Importantly, I learned that supporting children should not include advancing falsehoods on talent, ability, or quality of work. Raising smart children requires a partnership amongst the adults in their lives. Let's agree as educators and parents to do what's in the best interest of the child.

I started my teaching career in private schools. There, I saw firsthand the fierce advocacy that parents have for their children—not always on point, but passionate nonetheless. Thinking back to when I was teaching in the classroom, I wish I had this book to share and recommend to parents, to encourage them to see the benefits of allowing their children to earn their grades honestly and understand the importance of hard work.

I hope readers will use this to book to strengthen their parenting skills and improve how they advocate for their children. We can raise smart and successful young people if we embrace the strategies outlined by Meredith. Being attentive, listening, and talking with our children is the best way to help, encourage, and engage them. We must prioritize our children, make it about the child and not the image of the parent, or what someone else will think. We must set boundaries and realistic goals, and accept and love children as they learn and grow.

—Sheryl Davis, Executive Director, San Francisco Human Rights Commission

PROLOGUE

I never thought I would end up being a teacher. I had visions of moving to New York and writing for *Vogue*, and came to teaching totally by accident. I was working as an event planner and fundraiser in collegiate and secondary institutions when my life changed. It was a fluke. It was the best fluke that happened to me.

Now that I've worked in education—as a teacher for nine years and a principal for four years—I can tell you that educating children is what energizes me and gives me hope for the world. For the record, I am not a parent (yet). Yes, I know what you might be thinking: "Meredith is writing a parenting guide . . . and she doesn't even have kids!"

Very true. This is also true: Teachers these days often spend more time with your children than you do. I know that raising kids is hard. I know that kids can be both elating and frustrating. I know the sense of pride that comes when a student accomplishes something that they never have attempted before. I also know the heartache that pangs when they veer off course, squandering natural ability, potential, and the opportunity to grow.

I wrote this book with one intention: to help teachers and parents work together. We need to cheer each other on. We need to be each other's champions. We also need to talk about what's working—and what's not. We need to communicate with each other and with our students—your children—authentically and transparently.

We need to stop pointing out each other's flaws, but instead, let kids know they are supported by a village that is rooted in wisdom and best intentions. I hope this book enables teachers, parents, and students alike, to encourage one another. Not because test scores are up or discipline is easier, but because we are supporting one another seamlessly from home to school and back again.

Like you, I often second guess myself. I replay my days and ask myself:

- Did I make the right call regarding that discipline issue?
- Was my homework rigorous enough?
- Did I approach that conversation with authenticity?
- Why didn't that assignment resonate better with my students?
- Am I making a difference?

At school, I deal with the same challenges parents do: vomiting in the classroom, fighting on the play yard, talking back and telling me they hate me.

At the end of the day, I know that my students—your children—don't need us to be perfect. If you chastise yourself and question your every decision, you're not really present. I get it. But children need their parents and teachers to show up, to be there for them, to let them know they're safe.

My mom always told me I would be a good teacher, but in all honesty, I didn't think that teachers made enough money or had much of a social life. As a kid, I used to picture my teachers going home to a dark house—they sat in a plaid armchair with chocolate brown bookshelves, packed to the gills with old English texts, flanking their backdrop. There was a single amber floor lamp next to them, illuminated, as they graded papers. An afghan draped over their legs, their lives seemed lonely and desolate. So, no—I didn't see that same life for myself.

My time in education has spanned all grade levels, from elementary through college. I have worked with students of all ages, backgrounds, and personalities. I have taught, comforted, scolded, and advised them. I have graded papers, settled arguments, broken up fights, repaired relationships, bandaged scraped knees, and mended broken hearts. But in the end, middle school is where I landed, and the truth is, my life as a teacher and educator has been vibrant.

It is electric when you witness growth and progress in your students. It is life-giving—not life-draining—to plan and execute lessons, go into a classroom on the weekend to reimagine a bulletin board or decorate for an Election Day simulation, or put notes of affirmation in every student's desk. I was—and I am today—my best self when I am teaching.

Something you should know is that my mom was right—I should have been a teacher, and I am grateful that I am.

CHAPTER ONE
THE STARTING LINE: FIRST YEAR, OUT OF THE BOX

The truth is, I wanted to quit teaching halfway through my first year.

One day, about a month and a half into said first year as a seventh-grade teacher in Menlo Park, California, the mother of one of my students approached me. I was cleaning my classroom after a particularly tough day, and I was in the back of the room, straightening up—putting chairs up on student desks. She asked if we could talk. "I have been elected by the parents to tell you that we think you are too young, too green, and totally unfit to teach our children."

"Maybe you'd be better suited for kindergarten instead of seventh grade."

Kindergarten? I was stunned. Gobsmacked. Absolutely leveled. I mean, I knew that I was a fledgling—what new teacher doesn't? But better suited for kindergarten? I was killing myself taking work home at night, on the weekends, coming in on Saturdays and Sundays to ready my classroom in anticipation for the week ahead. All so that I could prove my passion and capabilities to students who pranked me and parents who doubted me. I was in my twenties at the time—certainly not the youngest on my faculty by any means—and I believed that youth was to my advantage—I still do, even as a principal.

I smiled, nodded, and thanked her for her candor. Then, after she left, I sobbed in the corner and wondered how I could possibly salvage this clearly ill-conceived occupational decision I had made to teach seventh grade.

And that's how my career as a teacher began.

First year, out of the box, idealistic, and in the lion's den of private school parents, I was blasted from all sides. Harsh emails, even harsher meetings and conversations, falsities told by my students to their parents taken at their very word; it all left me wondering—when did the universe shift so that teachers are the ones at fault while the students wield all the power?

I felt like I was drowning most days. The parents of my first class thought I was too young and inexperienced to teach middle school; my middle school students could smell my fear and apprehension and idealism from miles away, and they preyed upon that. My colleagues pariahed me—I was the black sheep, always late for classroom rotations, always behind on deadlines, and don't get me started on the trail of glitter and noise and chaos that I left in my wake.

When it came time for contracts to be renewed that spring, let's just say that I was convinced I was going to be looking for a new job.

But I didn't have to. And nobody knows how grateful I am for that. I have absolute appreciation for the administrator who took a chance on me, who extended to me the grace I needed to survive, who knew that nothing about working with kids is ever easy or how we envision it in our minds. Who recognized that I just needed time to get my sea legs and the rest would follow suit.

On Friday, December 14, 2012, one of the nation's greatest tragedies to hit a school took place—the shooting in Newtown, CT, where twenty children and six teachers were killed at the hands of a lone gunman. It was a moment that rattled the nation, yes, but one that sent a whole different shock wave through the hearts and minds of educators everywhere. Still teaching middle school language arts at the time, I recall being incredibly conflicted about the unfolding events. How is this happening? How do I tell my students? Do I say anything at all to them? And though I was struck with a fear so deep that I still could, if I let myself, shake throughout my days, I was more attuned to the fear and stress and anguish something like this causes our children. Because today's world is not the one in which you and I grew up. Today is not the age of innocence and childhood wonder that it once was. Today is not when adults carry the weight of the world while children laugh and play and live in the wonderment of life itself. Today is an overflowing bucket of stress for your child on levels you will never understand unless you try.

The outside pressures of today's society place an enormous burden upon today's children. They are bombarded on all sides with expectations: from you, from coaches, from friends, from teachers, even from the media. There's no longer time to simply be; instead, we overprogram, overwhelm, overschedule, overstimulate our overachieving students until they are fashioned into what the world wants them to be versus who they actually are. From the womb, we have created expectations that the right preschool will lead them to the right elementary school which will inevitably prepare them for the perfect high school because everyone claims that the perfect college is solely based upon this. Then it's the perfect job with the perfect spouse and their own perfect children, thus completing the trifecta of the square-peg-in-a-round-hole syndrome we have come to perfectly perpetuate on today's child. As I have said countless times, children are not perfect.

However, the problem is that, despite their flaws and shortcomings, children don't stop seeking to be so. They want to please you. They desire to be perfect in your eyes. They seek to postulate an aurora of flawlessness in front of a digital audience, most of whom have never before met them. But at what cost? You read the stories, you hear the headlines, you may even know of someone else's child, perhaps even your own, finding destructive ways to deal with the stress and pressure of the demands placed upon them.

Self-harm, whether in the form of cutting or purging or drinking or violence, is rampant among our youth. And I will circle back to this topic to explore it further, because I have been both participant in and witness to egregious actions done to oneself as a means of dealing with mounting outside pressures. For my students, I have seen everything from anorexia and bulimia to cutting to simply giving up and throwing in the towel of defeat because they can't measure up. I don't know which of these is worse, for they are all evidence that something in our rearing is wrong.

I often tell people that some of my greatest lesson inspirations would come to me at the most random times. Often they would be in response to an incident, like the Newtown school shooting. Other times, a news article read in the morning before my feet hit the floor often served as an expository writing prompt. Perhaps a song lyric wafting from my car's radio on the commute into work would turn into a five-paragraph narrative project. I would seize these creative bursts as a signal to pivot from my day's lesson plan and instead embrace a teachable moment. On one particular day, the lyrics came from Metric's "Breathing Underwater."

I gave a writing assignment to one of my English classes. They were to use this song as inspiration for a reflective narrative—to interpret either the theme of the whole song or to home in on one or two lyrics in particular. When they were handed in, two of the papers focused on the same theme: cutting, and not the type that is generally defined as skipping school. No, this cutting is when an individual uses any sharp object—a razor, scissors, a knife—to make cuts on their skin. The cuts can be in any area, and some are deeper and more aggravated than others.

The topics of these papers seemed terribly coincidental, especially considering that it was a class of fewer than thirty students. I pulled one of the two aside.

I began the conversation praising her essay, letting her know that I, first and foremost, was proud of her work. Giving praise often diffuses a tough conversation with your child, allowing them to immediately let down their guard and defense simply because you have given them the positive reinforcement that they are "good enough."

I went on to tell her that I was surprised that two papers were written from the same perspective and theme. She knew of whom I was referring and through gentle encouragement, she divulged to me that three of her classmates were harming themselves—cutting. What she didn't know was that I was already aware of another student in the class doing the same thing, bringing the victim count to four. Four! In a class of twenty or so students, four were seeking an alternative, unhealthy means of release. And this is not an isolated case. What may seem taboo to the well-adjusted adult is becoming more and more normal for our students today. They are so buried trying to be everything that everyone demands of them, it is no wonder that they seek an outlet to release, to let off a little steam.

Your students are not living in vacuums. They are exposed to the news, content, dialogue, discussions, and jargon that are sometimes disturbing, mortifying, even terrifying. Online channels, many deemed safe for youthful consumption, have covert messages that celebrate self-harm. Internet scams like the 2018 Momo Challenge or 2013's #CutForBeiber encourage students to hurt themselves or others. Innocuous lunchroom table conversations can morph in an instant from talking about what they have for homework that night or their favorite YouTube influencer to casual sex and kill lists and suicide. You cannot shelter your child, or yourself, from the reality that mature content, far beyond what they are developmentally ready to process, is part of the tapestry of their day-to-day. How are you helping them navigate those moments?

Are you listening?

Are you looking?

When tragedy breaks, I have found that the best way to address it is head-on. Whether it is a school shooting, sex ed, or an incident that affects only the minutiae of our school community, I have always used the foundation of honest dialogue to broach uncomfortable conversations. If we assume that someone else is going to tell our students what they need to hear, they will be left with nothing more than radio silence. I begin every conversation with facts. This is what happened. This is what we know. This is how I am feeling about it. How about you?

A colleague and I were talking about how it seems that a trend in education over the years has been to move away from owning our feelings. We have strayed from saying things to our students like, "I am angry" or "I am annoyed" to somehow presenting ourselves as emotionally neutral. But what does this teach our students? It definitely doesn't make us healthy communicators, and it certainly doesn't help our kids know that reactions and feelings are normal and worthy of being talked about.

If we want our children to be able to vocalize how they are feeling—to own the humanity of their emotions, their opinions, their fears, and views of the world—then we have to model how to do this, and do it well.

- "I am feeling sad because what you just said [to me, to a friend, to a sibling, etc.] was unkind."

- "When you ignore my request for personal space, I feel annoyed."

- "It makes me feel angry when you don't respect our shared class-room environment."

- "I feel jealous when someone else has something that I want. How about you?"

- "The loud commotion of everyone talking over each other right now is making me feel irritated."

Just as I have always used youth to my advantage with regards to relatability, vulnerability of feelings and emotions can achieve the same thing. I have told my students that I am afraid; that I am sad; that I am confused by situations or circumstances. Those are the human qualities that we all share, and by me giving them permission to feel those emotions, they are better able to own their insecurities.

But I don't stop there. I reassure them, too. I let them know that they are in a safe space where their feelings are valid and their fears are heard. I use facts to anchor their confidence in that which protects them—describing our school's safety plan; the stability they possess with their parents, guardians, or friends; and highlighting the qualities that make them the amazing students they are. No matter what the fear or insecurity they describe, I am ready to respond with a verbal life preserver and a physical presence that lets them know that I am here.

How about you?

CHAPTER TWO
KEEPIN' IT CLASSY

My first year teaching, I was trying to establish myself in my new school community. Sure, my seventh-grade students were making it very difficult to form a rapport with them, but surely I could connect with students in other grades. Right? As is customary, teachers, outside of their classroom responsibilities, also help with other campus needs—student council moderator, sports coach, PTA liaison. On this particular day, I was on the recess yard providing supervision, and I said "Hello" to a young student on the play yard. They happened to be the sibling of one of my pupils. Up until this point, we had always had a friendly relationship, talking during recess about shoes, favorite colors, and book characters. But on this day they said, "I'm not allowed to talk to you anymore. My mom doesn't want me to."

I was devastated, completely flabbergasted by this response. I couldn't imagine that this student had been privy to the conflict between myself and her mom—a disagreement over the rigor of my math instruction which, by the end of the year, was fully resolved and resulted in a supportive relationship that thrives to this day. But in that moment the truth was that clearly this child had been brought into grown-up conversations that permeated her young world and put up a wall between our school rapport.

Another time, a student in my class said to me, very causally I might add, in the middle of the school hallway as we were walking outside for dismissal, that his parents told him that I was anorexic. "You have an eating disorder, right?"

One morning, early in the year, a parent interrupted my grammar lesson to confront me about a story going around that I had made out with the Spanish teacher in front of their child's class.

And, there was the constant speculation that I was leaving midyear as I was pregnant with twins.

Educators encounter situations of student-to-student gossip, rumor, and bullying daily. But sometimes the beehive is buzzing more because of parents' doing more than that of the students. How do you handle your conversations with the parents whose company you enjoy? What about your relationship with those who annoy you? When you are privy to news about another family, witness drama in another family's life, what do you do? In two out of three of these scenarios, your answer should be to simply say nothing at all.

That's what I did in each of the instances above. I always responded with truth—"No, I am not pregnant." "No, I am not in a romantic relationship with a coworker." "I would be happy to speak with your mom and dad about my physical appearance if they would like." And, "Wow—I am really sad that your mom doesn't want us to talk at recess anymore." But beyond that, I left all gossip where it should be. Silent—no oxygen continually giving it life. No defensiveness to somehow fuel ongoing speculation. Just silence.

What do you do in situations like this?

I have made it my mission as a teacher, and now administrator, to expect from my students that they act with kindness and compassion, integrity, and character. Gossip within my classroom was unacceptable, as were idle rumors and stories that served no purpose other than to place said subject in a compromising light. In fact, my go-to strategy as both a teacher and a principal is whenever any student speaks negatively about either themselves (self-deprecation) or others, to have them write twenty-five positive adjectives for that person.

To be honest, I cannot recall what was the catalyst for the formulation of this strategy. Was it the panic I had and still have over how students treat one another? How we, as humans, are so ready with criticism for ourselves or those we encounter? Was it the need to increase my students' capacity for academic vocabulary and a cache of synonyms at the ready? Let's just call it D) all of the above.

"You're an idiot." Twenty-five positive adjectives about that classmate's intelligence.

  • You are smart, keen, wise, etc.

"I hate my hair." Twenty-five positive adjectives for how beautiful you are.

  • I am lovely, beautiful, tenacious, independent, etc.

"She's such a bitch." Twenty-five positive adjectives for that student's personality.

  • She is strong-minded, well-educated, astute, etc.

"I don't want them in my group." Twenty-five positive adjectives about inclusion.

  • We are a community of diversity, originality, creativity, thoughtfulness, etc.

"I'm so fat." Twenty-five positive adjectives how wonderful you are.

- I am determined, strong-willed, persistent, picturesque, etc.

Sure, they huff and sigh and roll their eyes, but it's a great way for them to drown out negativity with a focus instead on the positive qualities of others. Plus it's never a bad idea to put students in front of a thesaurus—the overt building of vocabulary becomes more and more essential in this digital age of abbreviations and emojis.

It's far easier to control community within the walls of my school. When students go home with their parents, that's it for me. My narrative is silenced and my expectations snuffed out until I am back in the classroom with them the next day. So the big question that plagues most teachers is: How do I combat the divisiveness that stems from the home? How do I counteract negativity between one student and another when their opinions are formulated by their parents' inability to keep their own comments and feelings in check?

You've heard the saying, "Little pitchers have big ears." I'm not sure truer words have been spoken. It may be difficult for your child to memorize the names of the states, or to learn what they need to pass an upcoming spelling test, but I promise you that they have no difficulty perceiving and absorbing every speck of detail when it comes to news about their classmates.

I've watched many parents pursue friendships with their children over the more traditional boundaries of parent-to-child rapport; students are exposed to dialogue and content that is often inappropriate for their developmental level.

I had one student who always knew everything about her mom's dating life—who the men were, what she and her boyfriends did together, the drinks they consumed, the parties they threw—she could recount every detail. Another kiddo could recollect every time their dad was inebriated and would, very jadedly I might add, both joke about and scoff at his drunken antics. I've known parents who kept their children home every time they themselves were "sick" or had something else to do, thereby leaving my students at home to miss day upon day of learning, only to come back to school with no explanation other than "My [parent] didn't want to bring me" for why they were absent.

Your children are not your peers, and you should never think it acceptable to gossip in front of them, chitchat with them, or enable them to pick up your habits; nor is it OK to channel your feelings of those in their class to them. I beg you—let them form their own opinions, make up their own minds, seek to accept everyone around them without finding fault or passing judgment in the immediate.

A few years ago, in the burgeoning time of social media, the parents in several classrooms at my school set up Yahoo groups. These were initially conceptualized as a means of disseminating information to one another more quickly, whether to arrange chaperones for a class party or to find a substitute for yard duty. One would expect that a group of adults, peppered with professionals and high-powered executives and stay-at-home-moms, would be able to adequately handle their social media exposure. But it didn't take long for this parent Yahoo group to veer from test prep, homework study sessions, and discussions of who would bring Rice Krispies treats to the game on Saturday to cattiness, gossip, rumor, and smack-talking about one another and other people's children. This led my administrator to shut down the Yahoo group altogether.

The problem with the group was twofold. First, humiliating, ostracizing, bullying, and trolling in any way—in person or via social media—is unacceptable. Second, these parents weren't simply using the Internet to tear one another down; they went one step further and told their children what they thought of both their classmates and their parents. So the children were coming to school day after day repeating verbatim what their parents said. "My mom said that I can't play with you." "My parents told me that you're a bad person." "My mom hates your mom." "Your dad drinks way too much."

My question is why are we, as adults, so desperate for an audience that we will willingly poison one child against another? Why do we keep missing the memo on raising children of tolerance, compassion, and empathy? We lead by example. Don't put your hand on the stove if you don't want your child to get burned. Little pitchers have big ears (and eyes). They see our side-eye glances toward others. They mimic our mannerisms. They drop f-bombs because we do. They absorb every word that we say; observe every hand gesture we give; can recount every expletive we mutter. As much as you filter photos on your Instagram feed—filter what you say and do in front of your children.

I received an email, sent to myself and a group of teachers, from a parent who wanted to "inform" us that their child was going to be a bit emotional for the first few days of class as they had experienced a trying weekend. That, in and of itself, would have been sufficient—a simple note letting us know that their student needed to be shown an extra amount of grace and asking us to consider accommodating their strife. The problem was that the email went on to describe why this student was upset, that they had witnessed a scandalous situation with another family, placing that family's mother in jeopardy. Names, dates, and details, all there in black-and-white—anonymity gone and opinions formed. Suddenly, the nonjudgmental perception demanded of our profession was shattered by one mother who had far too much time and far too little discretion on her hands.

AS MUCH AS YOU FILTER
PHOTOS ON YOUR
INSTAGRAM FEED—
FILTER WHAT YOU SAY
AND DO IN FRONT OF
YOUR CHILDREN.

Now I ask you—why describe the incident? Why subject a teacher's objectivity to information that holds no bearing on our ability to educate and nurture in an unbiased manner? As I have told so many students' parents over the years—leave the informing to the school's administrator. It is not your job as a parent to keep the teachers up-to-date on the scandals within the school's social circle. It is not your job to fill us in on who's doing what or doing whom. When you choose to disseminate irrelevant information to the faculty and staff of your school community, you are hindering their ability to do their jobs as effectively as possible. You are leading them to not only pass judgment on other students in the class, but also, your own. We are like any other member of the human race—we are subject to making assumptions.

So ask yourself if your own actions within your school community are causing faculty and administrators to pass judgment on you, your kids, and your family as a whole. Because as unfortunate as it sounds, it was nearly impossible for me as a teacher to look at a student without criticism when their parent had wreaked havoc on the tranquility of our educational environment.

The culprit is the rumor mill that festers within school communities, office dynamics, even social gatherings, creating an undercurrent of malice and leaving a wake of lost community. So what's the solution? A meme from social media influencer Kid President reads: "Give people high fives just for getting out of bed; being a person is hard sometimes." How do we reserve judgment of others and choose respect over critique? Let's work together to use our respective communities to increase the scope of our empathy, compassion, and collaboration. It's hard to be a grown-up—let's show our students how it's done right.

I believe the general consensus among educators is that at the end of each year, we want our students to leave as not only their best learners, but also, as their best selves.

A RESPONSIBLE SOCIAL PRESENCE

As we encourage our children to utilize social media in responsible ways, so too, do we need to hold ourselves accountable. We cannot chastise our kids for hiding behind the anonymity of a screen and then find one another convicted of the same.

Let me elaborate: Like anyone who maintains a digital presence, schools are certainly the recipients of online goading. Parents and guardians, bent out of shape over a meeting that didn't go their way or school policies that limit their power of persuasion take to the Internet's channels to air their grievances. Yelp reviews that are laced with venom and Great Schools posts created in a vacuum of momentary discontent create a ripple of discord that can be incredibly destructive to community. And, rarely is there a situation or circumstance that warrants taking down an entire school's reputation because you are finding yourself in a moment of upset or flat out having a bad day.

It is human nature to disagree; it is normal to have a difference of opinion or feel frustrated when things don't appear to favor our own desires. But, as much as it is inappropriate for our kids to impulsively lash out at friends or strangers online, we have to make certain that we are modeling cool, calm, and collective means of communication when we are feeling discontent. So, make an appointment to talk with your school's administrator. Set up a time for an authentic discussion with your child's teacher. Invite the fellow parent who has rubbed you the wrong way for coffee to find connection amidst your differences.

Set the tone and model for your kids the proactive, responsible way to communicate impactfully.

CHAPTER THREE
THE THIN RED LINE

A teacher's job is never done. I used to cringe when papers were returned and grades were posted, because I knew that the battle over why the grades assigned were what they were, the excuses for why a student didn't complete an assignment fully, or the demand for a change in grading policy was forthcoming.

I'm not alone here. Educators across grade levels and school districts share this feeling of panic. After all, the inbox of a teacher is never empty, always growing, forever incomplete. The mountain of papers, tests, quizzes, notebooks, Google Docs is an ongoing testament to knowledge acquired and comprehension garnered. We can come in early, work through lunch, leave late accompanied by a bag stuffed to the brim with paperwork, and still there are tasks that remain.

Granted, this is all part of the job. I've made it clear in this book how much I love teaching and being a school administrator. I am not naysaying the nuances of my profession. But despite how thrilled I feel when the clutter is purged and the papers I so tediously graded, edited, and scored have gone home, I know the work is never over. The emails will slowly flood my inbox again, the meeting requests will begin to sound, and the following day, I am sure to be ambushed by several parents, all clamoring to tell me the same exact thing.

"How dare you!" "Who do you think you are?" "My child's self-esteem will never recover." "Do you see how upset they are?" "My child knows how to write!" "I know their paper was good. I typed it for them!"

I remember one such encounter, toward the end of my first quarter as a teacher. I had edited three grades' worth of essays—sixth, seventh, and eighth—and, I passed them back to their respective authors one Friday afternoon. But before I had even exited the building to walk my class outside, I was greeted by one parent in particular, literally charging at me, essay in hand, student trailing behind them in absolute mortification. The parent went off on a tirade, stating that my grading criteria were clearly ill-informed, that my predecessor never gave her child anything lower than an A ever, and I had single-handedly ruined her child's confidence as a student.

Looking back on it, this was a turning point for me as an educator. Sure, I was rattled by this parent's skepticism, and I definitely questioned, once again, if I had what it takes to be an effective teacher. But I realized in that moment that this parent and I were both working toward the same goal. We just couldn't see our alignment at that time.

What I should have said then but need you to know now is that just like you, teachers see the best in your child. We see their aptitude for numbers and their talents as an author. We see their eyes light up when we mention the word *basketball* and watch as their synapses fire during an art lesson. We help ease their heartache when they lose a game, bomb a test, or make a poor decision. What I want you to know is that your child is not perfect—and that's absolutely alright.

It's essential that we rely upon our own experiences and memories during times when our children aren't perfect. Think back to when you were a child. Teachers were trusted to do their best by the child. But what worries me is that we have blurred the line between what is indeed best for the child, and what looks instead more like stroked egos and inflated grades. I have watched it happen: A student only learns apathy and lethargy and dependence on laziness and the direction of others if they have no goals, nothing for which to work and strive and achieve. We—I as teacher and you as parent—should never be in the position of diminishing their self-reliance and autonomy simply because their process of growing is a messy, complicated, bumpy road. Instead, let's join forces and champion them in moments of weakness.

During another noteworthy quarter, I recall that a strong student's grade in my English class had dipped. This overachiever had let careless mistakes and shoddy detail in their work overtake what was usually letter-perfect compositions and assignments. The C was well-deserved . . . and earned. Two days before said quarter's end, the parents found it imperative to question the whys and hows of their student's grade being less than exemplary. (Note: There is absolutely nothing wrong with this! Teachers want to have these conversations— open dialogues with parents and guardians in collaboration about the progress of our students.)

I firmly believe in meeting in person for conversations that are in any way tumultuous. I advise my colleagues, and try to hold myself to the same benchmark, that if an email requires more than three to four sentences of explanation on any given issue, they should sit down together, face-to-face, and talk it out. Emails and text messages—they are just words on a screen, devoid of vocal intonations or facial expressions to qualify the tone or intention of the correspondence. If we really want to achieve teamwork, we need to be in the same space and time, engaging in authentic conversation.

I recommend this strategy to my students, too.

So taking my own advice, the student's parents and I sat down together one morning before school began, and from the moment they walked in, the tension was palpable. They were clearly angry. I am an optimist by nature, and I always aim to approach difficult conversations as what a colleague of mine would describe as a "criticism sandwich": Start with something positive, get into the difficult meat of the issue at hand, and then conclude with forward-thinking goals and anticipated outcomes.

When I explained that things as simple as missed punctuation can devastate one's grade, I assumed that we'd have a constructive conversation about helping this student in the future.

Instead, they reacted with contempt. "You mean to tell me that [my child's] grade dropped from an A to a C because of periods?"

"Yes," I responded. This was, after all, an English class.

Teachers give grades to reflect not only achievement, but also to communicate how a child is responding to the academic material. However, they are the child's grades. These letters, scores, and percentages are not meant to be used as weaponry against the educator or the curriculum.

It's strange, but I have mastered the ability to discern what work has been written by my students, and what work is that creative genius of someone else. Call it intuition, call it a sixth sense, call it Google. But no matter what, call it plagiarism. You are doing your child no favors by assisting them in writing and editing their work. There is a wide gap between making a few suggestions about their homework and doing it for them. The funny thing, though, is that their voice as an author and contributor reflects the difference.

Let me explain—when your child is asked to write a sentence or a paragraph in school, away from you and your adult mastery of vocabulary, they are left to their own devices. Their true knowledge and skill set are on display—authentically, honestly, in real time. There are generally errors, corrections, and suggestions in word usage, verb agreement, depth, and detail. So when that same student is asked to write a more lengthy paper at home and brings it in polished, perfect, with adjective use that surges off the college charts, well, that stands out. Don't fool them or yourselves—whether they copy a passage from the Internet or simply borrow your input, cheating is cheating is cheating. And the one who is really losing out is your student.

I once confronted a student whose paper was clearly not their own. This child, while an intelligent being, was not at a cognitive level to draft the observations made in this paper. When I asked them about it, they admitted that they had received help from several sources (i.e., Mom and Dad). So I told them that they would have to redo the paper, on their own volition, without any assistance at all if they wanted to receive anything more than a zero. They conceded. End of story, move on, lesson learned.

Well, not quite. I believe it crucial for educators to maintain a transparent

IF YOUR CHILD'S TEACHER
EMAILS OR CALLS YOU WITH
CONCERNS, PLEASE
LISTEN. . . . IF YOU LAUNCH
INTO A DEFENSIVE TIRADE,
WE'RE NOT WORKING
TOGETHER. LISTEN,
EVALUATE, COLLABORATE.

relationship with their students' parents. That means that I am upfront with them about the goings-on of their son or daughter, and likewise, they see that my intentions are clear and without malice. In that spirit, I emailed the student's parents to let them know we had a discussion about the plagiarized paper and the agreed-upon consequence, and asked for their support in reiterating the message of doing one's own work for one's own self at home later that evening.

You can imagine my surprise (or maybe you can't, depending on your frame of reference) when the parent emailed me right back to state that their child had "worked very hard" on that paper and had been suffering from being "overwhelmed by schoolwork." The message was clear—their academic indiscretion was my fault.

Instead of placing blame, I encourage you, as parents, to seize these incredible opportunities for communication with your child about their motivation, comprehension, and absorption of what is being taught day in and day out.

I have found that most parents panic at the end of the quarter or semester, only at that juncture realizing the state of their kids' grades. If you exercise consistency in communicating with your student about their academic progress, and assisting them on that journey, the chances of overwhelm come report card season will be far diminished. Here's a few well-oiled strategies:

Strategy #1: Review their homework with them at night.

Some teachers use apps for homework alerts and reminders—sign up for those. Or have your student use an old-fashioned planner in which to write down their assignments, as the kinesthetic activity of writing is proven to assist with retention of ideas (i.e., work out their memory muscles). Don't settle for your student telling you that they've "done all of their homework" or "don't have any tonight." Instead, take five to ten minutes and have them prove to you that they've completed it, and completed it well.

Strategy #2: Help them study.

Flashcards may seem antiquated in this digital age, but they actually are a tried-and-true method of helping your student commit vocabulary words or math facts to memory. Take this one step further and have them use those words in sentences or practice their number sense with skip counting, estimating, or applying their fact fluency to word problems.

Strategy #3: Encourage them to write.

I know a parent who works with students at the postgraduate level. One day we were talking about the emphasis that we, as a school, were placing on the written word for all students, kindergarten through eighth grade. She replied that she was appalled at how many graduate students were coming through her program not being able to write. "They literally don't know how to write a well-crafted paper."

Scary.

I beg you—please force your kids to write and write often. And cultivate their command of the written word by putting pen to paper. Don't have them outline and compose rough drafts on Google Docs, as the writing process is one that requires old school, ink-to-notebook writes and rewrites in order for them to hone their voice as an author. The tactile engagement of gripping a pen, forming letters, words, sentences on the lines of traditional wide- or college-ruled binder paper will make all the difference as they learn how to craft well-written, beautifully articulated compositions.

According to an article in *The Week*, "University of Wisconsin psychologist Virginia Berninger tested students in grades 2, 4, and 6, and found that they not only wrote faster by hand than by keyboard—but also generated more ideas when composing essays in longhand. In other research, Berninger shows that the sequential finger movements required to write by hand activate brain regions involved with thought, language, and short-term memory."

And data compiled by Indiana University School of Medicine learning specialist Patricia Ann Wade suggests much the same: "Writing entails using the hand and fingers to form letters . . . the sequential finger movements activate multiple regions of the brain associated with processing and remembering information."

Buy your child a journal. Have them write thank-you notes. After a vacation or a special occasion, have them narrate their memories. The more practice we can give them putting their thoughts, ideas, feelings, and facts on paper, especially without the use of emojis and "lol," the more their communication skills are going to improve.

Now, the caveat here goes back to the intention behind this book: We are a team. If I see that your student is taking one step backward after the two steps forward they achieved earlier in the year, it is my obligation to sound the alarms. If you notice that your child is coming home each day announcing confidently to the world that they have no homework, please shoot me an email to confirm that their claim to free time is accurate. If your child's teacher emails or calls you with concerns, please listen. It should not be that every teacher develops bleeding ulcers come report card season.

Collectively, we need to work together when and if your son or daughter decides to ease up on the gas and coast through a quarter or two. We need to work together to encourage them but to also establish a tenor of accountability.

It's time to wake up and smell the autonomy—there will be times when you, and I, have to let your child fail. Let them see that they must be self-reliant in order to foster within themselves a growth and development far beyond what any textbook, standard, or educator can convey. Let them assume control of the vehicle in making an appointment with their teacher for extra help on social studies; send an email when they are confused on the nightly homework; attend study hall at lunch or after school. If you jump in and launch into a defensive tirade, then we're not working together. Listen, evaluate, collaborate.

More than once, a parent has demanded that I change their child's grade. The scenario goes something like this: The parents contact the teacher first, and then move on to the principal, who then circles back to the teacher to discuss and/or instruct a change to their records.

As an administrator, I listen to all sides—the parents', the teacher's, and the data. But as a teacher, when the higher-ups are positioned between a rock and a check to their school's endowment, how am I supposed to be able to take the moral high ground?

I am an educator, one who by nature and trade is meant to educate the whole child. I taught lessons on grammar, vocabulary, and reading comprehension alongside morality, integrity, and character development. My students walked out of the door of my classroom understanding how they were expected to treat humanity with kindness, compassion, and respect. They knew, based upon lectures and lessons, that honesty is always the best policy. Think about it—honor codes from the highest learning institutions demand it of their admits. Corporations fail and executives go to jail when they lack it. Reliability and integrity are at the very core of my job as a teacher to mold and shape a child into their best self.

But, so often, the world doesn't share in that same belief. Take, for example, Operation Varsity Blues, the 2019 college admissions scandal. In this cautionary tale, which shines a large light on the issue of academic integrity, fifty people were indicted, and thirty-three of those were parents. Moms and dads who were so intensely focused on what they wanted for their children's futures that they allowed their pride and position amongst the country's elite to skew their own integrity. They entered a house of cards magically erected by William Rick Singer, founder of The Edge College & Career Network. Singer would, for the right price tag, enable the overindulgent parent the chance to feast upon a buffet of endless possibilities for their children: modified SAT scores, falsified athletic achievements, bogus awards doled out at nonexistent ceremonies, and a red carpet leading straight into their college of choice. How far we have strayed from integrity, work ethic, and an unwavering belief in our kids that through determination and tenacity they can achieve success.

I beg you—please don't put any teacher in the position of hypocrisy. It is grossly unfair, selfish, and disingenuous to force an educator to alter the grading scale simply to suit your own notions of what is deserved. If one day your client, whomever that is, walked into your office and demanded that you alter the way you do business with them, what would be your answer? Would you allow them to change company policy simply because of the power or money that they wield? And how would you feel if that client then went to your supervisor, manager, or VP, and made the same demands, overriding your authority in an area of your dedicated and well-informed expertise? Please don't tell me that you'd be fine with it, because the truth is that nobody likes to be intimidated, overrun, outnumbered, or backed into a corner shrouded with inequity. So why should your child's teacher be treated any other way?

Please believe me when I tell you that you are not doing your son or daughter any favors by forcing the hands of their teachers, demanding that their grades reflect your expectations instead of the reality of their achievement. These are the formative years—the time when your child is learning how to advocate for themselves, achieve for themselves, and understand for themselves the value of hard work, dedication, and motivation. Their sense of autonomy and self-reliance will be forever stunted if they do not learn the difference between grades earned and grades given. Don't stand in the way of your son or daughter being their own person.

So I refer back to my dilemma. What do I do when you, as the parent, make demands of me, the teacher, to lie and deceive? I, as teacher, explain the reasoning for why your son or daughter earned the grade that they did. And you, as parent, accept the grade that your student has earned. You may not like it, but honesty is, after all, the only way.

Does this mean that you have failed as a parent seeking to raise a high-achieving student? On the contrary, some of the best lessons my students have learned from my edits and comments and grades on their papers are that they have room to develop: opportunities for growth. I teach ethics alongside every lesson on punctuation, thesis statements, and hyperbole in literature. I instruct my students that in all circumstances, there is no place better to be than in the truth; that honesty prevails beyond all iniquity.

And isn't that what you would want me to teach them? To perpetuate a society of scoundrels who show blatant disregard for any moral code puts in jeopardy the very heart and soul of teaching—to mold and shape future generations to be better than their predecessors (aka you and me).

The loss in this moment, when I as the teacher am forced to change a grade, is not my bruised ego—I can take a good many hits on the chin. No—the loss is in the extension of learning that this student could have garnered if the conversation we had in class was echoed at home. That the ideas of doing one's own work, citing sources when information is borrowed from the hands of another, and celebrating the student's eventual ownness and responsibility would be messages far more solidified in a child's consciousness if the dialogue was twofold—at school and at home.

Here are some moments of true learning that can shape your child's coping strategies:

- Misjudging the time it takes to complete an assignment

- Struggling to learn something new

- Occasionally testing low

- Getting an essay returned with edits and corrections

These are the stepping-stones to deal with setbacks and shortcomings when your child enters adulthood. If you jump in every time your child falters, and you demand perfection, they will certainly be maladjusted to the reality of life's imperfections—a common trait shared among so many.

If and when your student comes home with less-than-ideal grades or poor classroom conduct, embrace these as moments to authentically communicate with your child:

- Find out what happened. Ask why they made certain choices.

- Ask about how they feel.

- Listen.

- Ponder with your child ways they could have handled the situation differently.

- Give them the space to be candid about their own failings.

When a student approaches me, long-faced and teary-eyed because they bombed an assignment, my first question, without fail, is "What could you have done differently?"

I don't cater to their self-pity, nor do I wale on them about being irresponsible and not meeting my expectations. Instead I allow them to reflect. I give them the opportunity to exercise accountability.

More often than not, the conversation goes to something like:

> "I shouldn't have watched Netflix last night and studied harder for my test."

> "I spent more time on YouTube than I did on my homework."

> "I should have started on that project two weeks ago when it was assigned."

Even if this is the answer that they know you want to hear, giving them the chance to speak, to own their actions, enables them to hear their voice and establish a sense of power and control. Because you want them to feel that they are in control of their education—that they are indeed the ones who are going to school each day, for eight hours at a time—it is truly about them.

At Back-to-School Night each year, I used to tell my parents that I would celebrate the accomplishments of only one individual in their households—their student's. I didn't and still don't want to know that the parent can write or do math. I only want to know that their child has owned their responsibilities as a student, done the work required of this role, and put forth the effort necessary to be graded accordingly. And win or lose, that moment of autonomy when a student advocates for their own educational goals, ambitions, and strivings, that is a measure of achievement which far exceeds any letter grade to which I could assign.

We have lost sight of the intangible—those necessary qualities of being a good human that were long ago paved over by data qualifiers, SAT scores, and numbers on a transcript. I can't quantify integrity, compassion, benevolence, or authenticity. But those are qualifiers of success that are just as essential for their victory in the world.

STRATEGIES FOR STAYING ON TOP
OF YOUR CHILDREN'S GRADES

Regularly check their school's online grading portal:
Know your family's password and routinely monitor your child's progress one to two times, weekly. Recognize, of course, that some weeks are busier and more hectic for your child's teacher than others, so don't panic if you don't always notice new grades entered into the system.

If your child's school doesn't have an online system, then talk to their teacher about sending progress reports home on a consistent basis (every few weeks) in order to monitor their grades routinely.

Buy them a planner:
Using a written planner for students as early as third grade can assist with children assuming academic independence. Additionally, the discipline of writing things down enables stronger comprehension.

Collaborate with your child's teacher to set the expectation that your child will write down their homework each day, thereby giving you documentation of what they need to complete each night.

Use this planner as a checklist to evaluate finished work.

Develop an organizational system:
Clutter can derail a child's ability to stay on top of their work. Work with them to come up with an organizational plan that feels accessible to their unique style and needs.
- Colored folders for completed work, undone work, etc.
- Binders with specifically labelled tabs according to their verbiage, not yours— it's their system and needs to feel accessible to them.
- A whiteboard to-do list in a common area of the house to help keep both you, as parent, in step with your child in seeing, visually, what needs to be done and when.
- Routine backpack purges and regular desk checks in their classroom (with their teacher's permission, of course).

Celebrate the wins.
- Kick it old school and hang outstanding work on the refrigerator.
- Leave words of encouragement in their lunchbox before a big test.
- Adhere a Post-it Note to their planner with an affirmation of pride for a job well done if they completed homework the night before without a fight.

Embrace teachable moments.
- Encourage the learning from their mistakes by having them correct wrong answers.
- Add to their weekly spelling list by throwing in words of your own choosing and drill them in the car or commute to and from school.
- Have them write, and write, and write.

CHAPTER FOUR
PREPARE TO PIVOT

As you know, my time in education has spanned all grade levels—from elementary through college—and in the end, middle school is where I landed. Believe it or not, I was thrilled to teach seventh grade.

Seventh grade is an incredible year of transition for students. Watching them really grow into their personalities; embrace their talents, interests, and hobbies; stretch their legs a little more regarding appropriate use of sarcasm and questioning social norms—it all takes place in seventh grade. And I love it. The whole middle school experience, really. It's an incredible honor to get to be right there in the game of a human being figuring out who they are meant to be.

Granted, it's a bumpy road, for middle school in many ways remains much the nightmare we all remember. The awkward body-changing experience you still recall is just as real today as it was ten . . . twenty . . . even fifty years ago. Because students are students. Sure, the pace of life, its fads and trends—those things come and go. But the acne, body odor, and bad attitudes? Those will always haunt the middle school years.

Being a seasoned junior high school teacher, I have honed the art of sarcasm and snark. Boys get a little mouthy come December, and the girls can take on quite the diva persona in early spring. You can literally set your watch to it. Call it a communication tool or simply a means of survival, but banter does exist within my classroom. Because if you don't know how to speak to kids, relate to them on their level, you will not reach them, no matter what age or grade they are. You have to draw them into your corner, allow them to live the illusion, if you will, that you get them, you understand what their life is like, you sympathize with the stress of their world. It is never going to amount to the stress and pressure you as a parent feel, but it is not their job to see the world through your eyes—they have no point of reference for that. But you do. You were them at one time, not too long ago. And even if it was longer than you'd like to admit, dust off the memories and fake it. Because you will get much further with your son or daughter and their attitude if put your disciplinarian demeanor on the back burner and freestyle a conversation with your student.

Pivot away from the typical question-and-answer sessions of "How was school?" and "What did you learn today?" because they won't take the bait. They have been routinized to navigate these questions with answers that will suffice in the moment, and their fear of both vulnerability and judgment can be paralyzing to them.

If you want to have meaningful relationships with your children, they must trust you to listen authentically, advise with compassion and not judgment, and validate them always as your treasured creation. You have to speak to them as though they matter. Their quirks, their smirks, and their insecurities all truly matter.

I once had a colleague pull me aside. He said that he had heard from a student what he thought was "the highest compliment that could be paid to a teacher":

"You know, when you are talking to Mrs. Essalat, you really feel like she is really listening to you."

I was overwhelmed but grateful that my efforts to relate to my students and connect with them on their individual levels was resonating. Is it my use of direct eye contact? Leaving my phone on the desk while they are speaking? Crouching down to make sure that we are talking on the same level? Aiming to balance my approach of both holding high expectations while celebrating mini-milestones along the way? Perhaps. But what I do know for certain is this: Our kids are craving for us to hang on their every word. To respond to their jokes, their attempts at sarcasm. To listen to them rant or blow things totally out of proportion. To validate them when they are feeling small and insignificant, and to talk them off the ledge of bravado.

Listening to your children is critical. First, they hunger for your attention, your approval, your interest. Even the most apathetic middle school student wants to know that their parents care about what they do. They want to know that even in their most frail moments, they are loved. So imagine, then, how crucial displaying this form of affection is to children in kindergarten or second grade, who are even newer, and fresher, and more vulnerably attached to the profound discoveries of who they are and of what they are capable.

I once asked one of my students why they rolled their eyes whenever their parent came to pick them up from school or drop off their lunch at noon. We were about to head outside for recess, and it seemed the perfect time to gain an understanding of her feelings.

So just as she was leaving the classroom, I asked if we could chat for a few minutes. I have found that unless you want a student to sit and stir about a lie that they've told or get them to lower their defenses before confronting them about a serious offense, you catch them on the fly. Any more of a heads-up, in situations where you are striving to establish vulnerability, will only cause kids to clam up.

At first, I, too, got the roll. But I pressed further, asking more probing questions. Middle schoolers may have attitude, but they lack the willpower to hold out on any conversation for too long.

"No, really," I said. "I want to know."

"She just asks so many questions," was her response. "I just don't feel like answering the same thing every day."

"I totally get it," I said. "I used to feel the same way. It's so tough dealing with parents sometimes."

"Really?" she replied. She seemed a bit stunned, but her shoulders relaxed, and I could tell that we were making progress.

I continued: "Absolutely. I completely get where you're coming from. But, wow. Think of it this way: You have a mom who is willing to drop everything to take care of you. That's kind of amazing. You could be stuck eating the hot lunch from school, right? Or walking home?"

She responded, "That's true. I had the chicken nuggets last week, and they were awful!"

"I bet," I chuckled. "So what did your mom bring you today?"

"A salad and cookies," she responded.

"Nice!" I said.

"Yeah," she said. "I guess it is."

Now, I had two directions in which I could have taken this conversation. On one hand, I am her teacher in that moment, so I should teach her about respect and gratitude and call out her bad attitude while I'm at it. But instead I sat down with her, calmed her anxiety, and talked it out.

I began the dialogue acknowledging her feelings, justifying her belief that sometimes adults (and you know that we do this) are repetitive. We don't get the answer we like, so instead of changing our strategy, we simply say it again and again, louder and louder. Because you are a busy parent, who has a life and a job and a home to care for, bills to budget, and dinner to get on the table. And at the end of it all, you simply don't have the time or patience to think outside the box. I get it. So what do you do in that moment?

Most parents throw in the towel, or resort to fighting with their kids, repeating the same conflict and confrontation in which they engage day after day.

"How was school?"

"Fine."

"What did you learn today?"

"Nothing."

SOME DAYS COMMUNICATING WITH YOUR CHILD WORKS; OTHER DAYS MIGHT BE A BIT TOUGHER. BUT, TAKING THE TIME TO CHANGE HOW YOU BEGIN AND END CONVERSATIONS WILL MAKE A DIFFERENCE TO YOU AND THEM.

"How are your friends?"

"Fine."

"Do you have a lot of homework?"

"No."

"So tell me about your friends."

"God, Mom, stop!"

"Stop what?"

"You're always doing this!"

"Doing what?"

"This! Just . . . ugh!" (Cue eye rolling.)

Crickets.

It's all about perspective. When we get creative and navigate away from the usual dialogue we've established with our kids, we gain perspective on their circumstances. And they, too, gain perspective on ours.

Some days communicating with your child works; other days might be a bit tougher. But taking the time to change how you begin and end conversations will make a difference to you and them.

CONVERSATION STARTERS

Ask questions of your kids that are open-ended and require them to give more than a one-word response. Drive them away from the typical "Yes," "No," "Nothing," and "Fine" answers, and instead prompt them to dive into detail.

- What was one great thing that happened for you today?
- Tell me about (example: math, social studies, reading, art, P.E., etc.) class today.
- What's one thing that you like best about your school?
- What was the hardest question on your science test?
- What was something difficult that you tackled today?
- How did you take advantage of the opportunities offered to you today?

CHAPTER FIVE
NOT ANOTHER FACE(BOOK) IN THE CROWD

In today's age, your child most likely has access to a cell phone, an iPad, a laptop, or a Chromebook. Even more likely is that your child already has their own set of devices. You have many reasons for this, I'm sure, like making certain that your child gets to and from school safely, stays in contact with you when they arrive home, has full access to information at the ready.

And they probably also have a social media account—more than one, most likely. TikTok, Snapchat, Instagram, YouTube?

But with each of these platforms, it's no longer just about messaging their friends or posting pictures of their favorite foods. You need to ask yourself:

- Are they sliding into strangers' DMs?

- Are they accepting the follow requests from an online community they know nothing about?

Even if you don't think they do, how are you certain? I'm often shocked to realize that so many parents don't know what their kids are browsing online, or who they're communicating with. I can't implore you enough to be aware of what your children are doing in the virtual world.

And this is where a teacher's insight comes into play. This is why we confiscate cell phones at the start of each day and return them only when students leave for the day. They are a distraction, yes. But they are also a vehicle to voyeurism, placing student safety at risk.

When your child gets home, trots to their room, shuts the door, and doesn't emerge until the smell of dinner wafts into their cavern, what are they doing? You assume homework, because, from our well-adjusted adult perspectives, that is the only logical conclusion. And that's what they tell you they're doing. So why wouldn't you believe them? But there is a whole wide web out there luring your child into infinite exploration.

Now, social media and technology are wonderful tools. Believe me, I can stalk on IG for hours on end. But sometimes too much information is just that: too much information. The Internet is unregulated, which means that anything someone wants to put out there goes out there, unfiltered and ready for human consumption. And much of that content is unsuitable for even the most mature of adults. But plant a tech-savvy preteen in front of the screen, and chaos is bound to ensue.

Children are curious. They have questions about sex, the news, life, and relationships.

And while some of those topics may make you feel a bit uncomfortable, what should really keep you up at night is who is answering those questions if you are not. How are they forming their ideas and opinions on sex, love, and dating? How are they getting their information about world conflict, violence in the United States, and crime in elementary schools just like theirs? How are they deciphering what is acceptable language and what certain slang terms mean?

Someone is going to teach your children about life. I implore you to be this person.

I had a student once use the N-word in my classroom. I should probably explain that it was in the context of a discussion about language and the transformation of words throughout history. This student brought up the use of the slang version of the N-word, often heard today in rap or hip-hop lyrics. I explained that this word was rooted in hatred and prejudice, and that now, even though it had become part of their musical reality, they needed to understand that the context of the word did not allow for it to take hold in their own dialogue and conversation.

I was grateful for this moment, the opportunity to clarify something very deep and consequential for this student. Imagine if they never had anyone tell them that that word was not meant to be part of their adolescent jargon? What consequences arise when we let the Internet, social media, even television teach our kids the life lessons they so desperately need to learn?

I've had numerous students use social media as a means of inciting violence against one another. Sometimes it's other students they know right there in our immediate community. Other times it's been students from other schools. Either way, the filter of a screen gives them a false sense of bravado—the uncanny ability to say things to others that they wouldn't have the gumption to do in person.

One middle schooler, in particular, went back and forth with a student from a neighboring school, threating to fight one another. What seemed like a benign comment at first, labeling their posted photograph as "stupid," turned into an all-out turf war, with a gathering of students from the other school literally beating down our front door looking to take on anyone willing to rumble.

Another student was using an app to goad students in our own school community to fight them, beginning by criticizing their physical appearance. Still others have used photos to "slut-shame" classmates—calling them out for rumored sexual indiscretions.

SOMEONE IS GOING TO
TEACH YOUR CHILDREN
ABOUT LIFE. I IMPLORE YOU
TO BE THIS PERSON.

I, too, was the victim of viral venom when a student used their cell phone, after school and without my knowledge, to film a disciplinary meeting between myself and their guardian, calling me a "ho" for their Snapchat followers to mock.

When I discovered each of these examples, I was shocked—for several reasons. First, I would never place any of these students as the kind who seeks to instigate the physical harm of another. But more than that, when I brought it to their guardians' attention, most of their responses didn't track with my dismay. For starters, they were unaware of both the app and their student's use of it. And, second—they really just wanted to chalk the whole thing up to hormones, to give their students a pass for their behavior based simply on the fact that they had been hormonal for awhile and that their posts and subsequent actions were somehow justifiable. They said that the other students involved had said some hurtful things, too, and that should somehow appease my upset at the potential harm these posts could have caused had it not been brought to my attention.

Tip #1: Establish screen time for your kids when they're online.

Monitor your students' use of the Internet. Oversee their Snapchat feed. Follow their Twitter activity. Check out their Instagram photos. See the TikTok videos they post and the follower requests that they receive. Stay on top of the new social media forums that burst forth into life daily; you must be one step ahead of your kids. I will repeat that: You must, at all times, stay one step ahead of your kids. They don't have to know that you know who they are playing Fortnite with. But the fact remains, you do and you're vigilant.

Tip #2: Please don't embarrass your kids on social media.

I once had a father call out his daughter on her YouTube channel. He wasn't happy with the content of her posts, so instead of having a one-to-one conversation at home with her, discussing back and forth, both his feelings and hers, he took it upon himself to publicly shame her. It backfired, and she became even more emboldened to keep up her online presence. Often this strategy can also encourage kids to find ways to be subversive—to hide their wheeling and dealing and completely uninvolve their parents.

That frightens me.

Those conversations do not need to involve a public forum. That is a surefire way to shut down the lines of communication—indefinitely. Instead, seek to put up incognito parameters and safety measures to assure that they are able to stretch their voices and autonomy and selves without jeopardizing their present or future reputations and opportunities.

Tip #3: Keep tabs on your kid's social media accounts.

It was brought to my attention that students had posted a picture on Instagram throwing up gang signs and wearing related paraphernalia. Two students—navy blue bandanas—fingers twisted to resemble a "W." Compound that with the fact that these pictures were taken on school property, after school, when their cell phones had been returned to them. And, one step further, that when I confronted their parents, while both sets were shocked, one of the student's guardians had no idea that this child had an Instagram account. That they had specifically told them that they were not to have an Instagram account. The news of this child's betrayal was almost as devastating to them as the content of the post itself.

When it was still a primary forum, I would occasionally check out my students' Facebook pages. Most of them did not put in place privacy settings, which meant that anyone could look at their pages—teachers, other parents, admissions counselors.

What I often found astounded me. On one occasion, I saw one of my seventh-grade boys in photographs making numerous sexual hand gestures among other things. When I spoke with his mom, she was flabbergasted. She said that she was certain her son didn't know what he was doing when he took those pictures, but I politely disagreed. She explained to me that their home environment was conservative—the children were not given "unsupervised freedom" to peruse the Internet, etc. without a guardian present. "I have no idea where [they] would have learned that!"

To be honest, I hear that often. That children's time spent online is in the company of a guardian. But I always press further. "Are you doing work while they are online?" "Is your iPhone, tablet, or laptop present when they are on their own device?" "Do they have a device in their room with them when they go to bed?" Because even though our physical bodies may be present when our students are following their own online routines, we are often distracted, disengaged, devoid of the presence of mind to notice when they click on a suggested YouTube video that potentially takes them down a rabbit hole of suggestive imagery and language. We don't mean to become preoccupied—it's just a result of our never-ending to-do list.

A fourth-grade student who lost computer privileges at school because they were sending sexually explicit messages to their online tutor; the seventh-grade student who copied their essay from SparkNotes and used words, when questioned, they couldn't define; the seven-year-old who whispered to another student to "suck my dick"; the cyberbullying and body shaming of one student to another through school email or Google Hangout. The students who think they are being coy with jargon that, when looked up on Urban Dictionary, would make most adults blush. No one wants to think of their student having the capacity of being in possession of mature content. But the tragic reality is, they do.

According to a ROX (Ruling Our Experiences) Research Brief, "In 6th grade, about 30 percent of girls report that most teens their age send sexually explicit texts and photos to one another. By 12th grade, this percentage rises to 75 percent, with two out of every three girls reporting that they have been asked to send a sexually explicit photo to another person."

Your children know way more than you give them credit for. Never make the mistake of assuming that they don't know what they are doing—they do. But often their young brains don't fully grasp the extent of their online content. They post and "like," they "poke" and accept the follow requests of total strangers, not seeing beyond that fleeting second of anonymity.

Young people are sometimes naïve to consequences; they act first, think later. They need to understand that once something is placed out there in cyberspace, it's permanent. They can try every which way to delete it, but those posts, pictures, and hashtags will forever be emblazoned upon their names and reputations.

Let your child know that you will be following them. That you will be monitoring their content in order to keep them safe. That you will not comment on their posts, nor will you engage their friends and followers in conversation. No, you are simply going to be a silent participant in order to stay involved in their digital life.

And always be sure to spot check their phones. Who is texting them? What kinds of pictures are they sending and being sent?

Tip #4: Your child's future is on the line.

A former student and I were having coffee a few days into her freshman year of high school, and when I asked how things were going, she told me about a classmate who had already been suspended. Suspended after only two days, I thought to myself. Turns out this student had posted several photos that were deemed scandalous by the school's administration, warranting disciplinary action. If it's out there, it is public domain. Anonymity is a concept we abandoned long ago.

You cannot assume that your child will somehow be more shielded than other children in your community. All kids are vulnerable to online predators; they are unaware that what they put out into the digital universe can never be erased. It can all be traced, tracked, and eventually, lead to trouble.

A 2017 article by Common Sense Media cites the following:

> According to the *New England Journal of Public Policy*, contact with online predators happens mostly in chat rooms, on social media, or in the chat feature of a multiplayer game.
>
> Only 5 percent of online predators pretend they're kids. Most reveal that they're older—which is especially appealing to twelve- to-fifteen-year-olds who are most often targeted.
>
> Teen boys who are questioning their sexuality are the second-most-targeted group because they often feel talking about it online is safer than sharing in real life.
>
> Teens want to feel special, validated, attractive, and understood at a time when they're separating from their parents, so an older "friend" who's very interested in them can feel exciting and special.

Additionally, schools and colleges have been known to "friend" potential applicants in an effort to better know their prospects. I am not condoning judgment on anyone's part, but the fact remains that your child will be judged based upon the persona they portray on the Internet. What would they find on your child's page that would lead school officials to question their character? Something as simple as a picture of your son or daughter drinking from a red plastic cup can lead to the assumption that they were engaged in underage consumption. Pictures posted of sexy smiles or funny hand gestures can lead some to question your child's morality. Really. I'm not kidding.

Tip #5: Talk with your child.

Talk to your child about what it means to safeguard their reputation, to be acutely aware of how others could perceive their actions, their posts, their comments. Let them know that they themselves are responsible for a large part of what other people will think of them—so they need to choose their actions, their friends, and their profile pictures wisely. Don't scorn them or make the conversation seem like a mandated laundry list of don'ts and more don'ts; instead, let them lead you in the discussion. Ask open-ended questions that do not interrogate but rather invigorate your communication with them. The safer they feel about being honest with you, the more you will know about them. And this knowledge is power.

Please talk to your kids about voyeurism and how to protect themselves from objectification.

I had a student once post a video of herself and her friends on TikTok during the school day. Outside of the fact that policy was broken by having a cell phone out on the recess yard, I was more concerned over the fact that these students were put in jeopardy. They admitted that they do not know every follower on their Snapchat, IG, and TikTok accounts. They don't have a benchmark for who these individuals are. I went on to tell them that by posting videos of themselves, wearing clothing with the name of the school blazoned on it, they were putting our entire community in jeopardy. What if one of these followers has a history of hurting children or attempts to take them from school? What if they somehow make their way to campus and leer at a playground full of young students? This is dark stuff, I know. But if our kids are feeling mature enough to put themselves out there to an audience of strangers, then they are mature enough to hear the potential ramifications.

I've always had the rule that my students were allowed to follow me on Instagram or Facebook after they had graduated. I am very judicious with what I post online, as I have always sought to make sure that I am practicing what I preach. Recently, however, I am rethinking following altogether, as it is really difficult to see students post more and more photos of themselves in compromising attire and positions. They have every right to stretch their autonomy and express themselves, but again, I have to wonder, given how scary our world has become, at what risk are we willing to cast off concern for what they put online?

When they post photos of plunging necklines, push-up bras, and thong bikinis, how are we able to protect them from online predation?

Common Sense Media has a few ideas for strengthening your child's resolve regarding their self-esteem, as well as how to establish a safe and strong online presence:

> Encourage your kids to get involved in positive, constructive online forums where they feel valued.

> Help your kid develop a healthy approach to social media so it's only one aspect of their lives.

> Choose quality media with diverse characters.

> Encourage social media breaks when online drama heats up.

The bottom line is this: Our kids need protection from an infinite cyberspace illuminated with deception, temptation, and the allure of anonymity. They need us, and the wisdom that we have to provide, in order to shield them from harm they don't even realize exists.

CHAPTER SIX
GET. A. HOBBY.

Let me pause here to express my gratitude and appreciation to you, the parents. Thank you for being so involved. Thank you for offering your assistance when we, the faculty, need it. There have been countless moments in my time as an educator when the parent populace has stepped forward to help me with a myriad of responsibilities: planning parties, driving on field trips, organizing supplies for projects and activities. It is definitely a necessity and a gift throughout the year when you arrive, ready and willing to pitch in and help.

OK—here's the caveat: There is a delicate balance between helping and hindering, assisting and assuming, stopping by and overstepping in. Sometimes, less is more becomes more is more and then, too much of it. The "it" to which I am referring is of course, parental overinvolvement, and it permeates today's school community. It seeps through the walls, the floors, the books, and the intercom. It faintly knocks, then barges through classroom doors at 7:58 a.m. when the bell is about to ring, and surges through emails at 11 p.m. Though it tries to disguise itself in benevolence, it's not fooling anyone, for it truly reeks of boredom and identities lost. This is the plight of the overinvolved parent and the overwhelmed teacher who has to deal with it.

Your children should absolutely and unequivocally be at the center of your universe. No one should take on the role of a parent without first and foremost agreeing to the terms and conditions of raising a child. Because despite what we all know to be true in raising a child, it often feels like there is no village. It is you, possibly a spouse, and them. Your children cannot take care of themselves, so they rely upon you as their constant source of transportation, food, money. You get them up, drive them to school, pick them up, take them to baseball, soccer, piano, and chess. Then you cook them dinner, prod them to do their homework, get them to bed, and finally, crash yourself before awaking the next morning to do it all over again. I get it. It's your world, and that's terrific. Job well done! And for some of you, that's enough. That's the extent of it. You have your own stuff to take care of in the moments of the day when your son or daughter is not with you, and you find that more than fulfilling. You have honed the art of maintaining your own identity in addition to the role that you assumed as parent. You don't have to drive on every field trip, you don't need to hang outside the door of the classroom before or after school chatting it up with other parents; you would be just fine letting the school do its thing and you do yours. Before I go on, if this is you . . . on behalf of teachers everywhere, I thank you.

Because many parents today have lost perspective. We are a society of extremes. There are those who do too little and those who do too much. Very few Goldilocks get the "just right" . . . well . . . right. And I am still not sure of which two extremes I would rather encounter as a teacher. I mean, the underinvolved parent is certainly the victim of fodder among the faculty. We roll our eyes at the mention of the name of that "absentee parent" who is always two steps behind the eight ball—the parent who forgets to pack the bag lunch on field trip day, so their child eats graham crackers out of their chaperone's car seat cushions. The parent who remembers after the school day is done that they were to supply two dozen cupcakes for the class's Valentine's Day party. The one who misses their parent-teacher conference, sends an email the morning report cards are distributed asking if their child can receive extra credit to bring their grades up, never insists upon their child wearing a jacket in the morning, or lets them ride their bikes home in a deluge of rainwater. Ah yes, those special cases.

But as much as I shake my head in bewilderment at their vacancy, I struggle with criticizing them. Because after all, isn't that what I am asking for?

I was having lunch one day with a colleague. Although it was summer vacation and despite our best efforts to talk about non-school related topics, the conversation found its way back to our favorite subject—kids.

"What's your neighborhood like?" I inquired. "Are there lots of families with kids?"

She went on to describe her next-door neighbor. Or rather—she went on to describe her next-door neighbor's nanny.

"I've never seen the dad with his kids. Ever." she recounted.

She said that she would see his two kids each day with their nanny, hear his car pull up at night, and watch the nanny leave. And then, the next morning, well before my friend would wake up her own children, back would arrive the nanny, followed by Dad headed out to work in the dark. Weekdays. Weekends. It didn't matter.

Sometimes, the mom would come and get the kids, but those visits, she recalled, were few and far between.

"So who is raising those boys?" I asked. Her response was simple: "The nanny."

She and I could conjecture, of course, all sorts of circumstances. Dad works two jobs. Mom travels most days. It was a contentious divorce with Dad getting the majority of custody without having the time to care for the children on his own. There were a myriad of possible explanations, and to be honest, we were not and are not owed an explanation.

YOU ARE NOT AT THE CORE
OF OUR UNIVERSE—YOUR
CHILD IS. AND THE
PARENT WHO IS *ALWAYS*
THERE ENDS UP HAMPERING
OUR BEST ENDEAVORS TO
PROVIDE THE BEST POSSIBLE
EDUCATION. . . .

. . . WHEN IT COMES TO THE SPEED BUMPS ALONG THEIR ROAD OF ACADEMIC, SOCIAL, AND EMOTIONAL EXPLORATION, PULL UP A LAWN CHAIR AND CHEER THEM ON FROM THE SIDELINES.

But we were left with just one question: If someone isn't going to make the time, have the time, spend the time with their own kids, then why have them at all? I've certainly encountered the parent who clearly had children because it was part of their life's checklist:

- College degree? Check.

- Six-figure job? Check.

- Perfect spouse? Check.

- Perfect home? Check.

- One dog, two kids? Check. Check. Check.

But life doesn't live in the extreme—and having kids is a far too all-encompassing privilege to limit it to a checklist or total absenteeism.

Child-raising shouldn't live on either end of the proverbial spectrum.

What's wrong with the middle? Balance, a happy medium, halfway between overbearing and underwhelming—that's a point of perfection. Parents, we teachers want to see you . . . once in a while. If a realtor had the same client sitting in their office day in and day out, or a server had their shift stifled by a patron following them around from table to table, it would become burdensome to say the least. You are not at the core of our universe—your child is. And the parent who is always there ends up hampering our best endeavors to provide the best possible education we can for your children.

Besides, when one parent seeks to carry the responsibility for every class party, every fundraising initiative, every issue of the school newspaper, and every PTA meeting, they diminish the amount of involvement required by the remaining 99 percent of the parent community. Raising a child truly does takes a village— we all know that to be true. But don't elect yourself to be chief of the tribe. Step back once in a while and let someone else take the lead.

I was speaking with a colleague on a day not unlike many other days, at the start of the week, when the kids were amped up and the teaching staff was exhausted. Every minor infraction seemed to become a major headache. We had a check-in meeting, and I asked her how the year was going.

She sighed. She went on to describe to me what I can only recount as commonplace— she was exhausted by telling her students what to do. She felt that she was in the never-ending rinse cycle of repeating her directions time after time after time. "I feel like I am saying the same thing over and over and over again to them. Why don't they listen to me the first time?" was all that she could ponder.

It was the beginning of the year and, as most teachers do, she was overexaggerating regimens and routines to enable a more streamlined year ahead. One such policy was the process by which students were to turn in their homework in the morning. She had gone over it day in and day out for the past two weeks. The catalyst for our conversation was when she noted that one second-grade student in particular stood at the homework basket for several minutes, paper dangling over the bin. She pivoted her head back and forth—from bin to teacher to bin to teacher and so on. My colleague was flabbergasted. "Just put your paper in the tray and head out to recess," she said. The student still looked pensive as she placed the paper into the receptacle and wandered outside.

This wasn't an isolated incident with only this student. Numerous children in her classroom were bewildered and perplexed as to what they were supposed to do when given explicit instructions.

Why indeed. Our conversation continued and the light bulb went on. We realized this:

Our students are unaccustomed to doing things for themselves. It's so challenging for them to think independently, and to act!

Why? I believe this is because parents, guardians, family, and friends carry the bulk of the burden for their kids, leaving them totally incapacitated when asked to do something on their own.

Parents, I know you mean well. I believe you are acting with incredible benevolence . . . but every time we swoop in to help our kids, we stifle their independence.

We should never stand by and watch as a child drowns (both literally and figuratively), but we also should never let them stay in the shallow end forever. I have watched parents come to school to spoon-feed their second-grade students at lunchtime. Watched them complete their projects, write their papers, solve their friendship flailings. But while these well-intentioned guardians think they are helping their kiddos, they are actually holding them back from reaching their capacity for figuring things out for themselves. Realizing their individual abilities for conflict resolution and self-sustenance.

Pick them up when they fall down. Put a Band-Aid on their broken hearts and salve on their scraped knees. But when it comes to the speed bumps along their road of academic, social, and emotional exploration, pull up a lawn chair and cheer them on from the sidelines. It's time for your kiddos to get in the game.

IDEAS FOR WELL-BALANCED PARENT INVOLVEMENT

Chaperone for one field trip per year and give other parents the chance to do the same.

Be a Room Parent: Help find field trip chaperones, plan holiday parties for the class, and assist the classroom teacher with communication around classroom happenings.

Attend regular PTA meetings to have a better understanding of what's going on in and around your school, network with other parents (especially those from other classrooms), and learn of ways to plug into the greater community.

Sign up for a Parent-Teacher Conference when prompted by the teacher.

Routinely check your child's grading portal and discuss with them, first, their grades.

If you need to speak with your child's teacher, arrange a time during their posted office hours or email them for a convenient time—do not bombard them before school or during dismissal, as these are harried and hectic times.

CHAPTER SEVEN
EYES WIDE OPEN

Now that I have your attention, I want to flip this and talk about students who really do need their parents to step in and support them unconditionally right now. These are the kids who are suffering, the ones who feel inadequate. These kids are hurting; they're so afraid of disappointing you and letting you down. These are the kids who turn to the blade of a razor, or knife, or a pair of scissors, to watch themselves bleed, if only from a single wound, a release from the mounting pressure suffocating their childhood.

I'm talking about self-harm, and as I said in chapter four, I have had more than several students confide in me that they were struggling with it. Cutting has become the next-gen source for relieving stress and anxiety. It's tragic, really, to think that these children are suffering so greatly from the expectations we, a society of overachieving, overworked, overstimulated, overscheduled perfectionists, are projecting to our youth—too fragile, innocent, and underdeveloped to know how to process said mandates.

I'm in awe of my students who've had the courage to come forth and own their struggles They're so brave. But sometimes there was a caveat to their admission—they pleaded for me not to tell their parents. They were terrified that their parents would be "disappointed" in them; that they would never again look at them in the same way. They verbalized that if their parents knew what they had been doing, they would cease to love them in the same fashion.

Now in a spirit of honesty, I had to tell these students that, yes, their parents may be disappointed. What parent wants to hear that their child has been struggling? What parent wants to know that their child, in secret, has sought destructive ways to cope? Information changes things. The more we learn, the more we know, the more our perceptions of the world and everyone in it changes. So yes, when a parent, or even me as the teacher, learns the dark secrets of a student's heart, it changes the way we all look at them. But as I told my students, this isn't a bad thing. I mean, if a parent or teacher was to scorn said student for their admission, shun them, berate them for their struggles, then that would be . . . inappropriate? Wrong? Bad. But if their admission and honesty and candor lead us to look at them with more respect, admiration, care, and concern, that is transformative. That builds trust, and healthy communication can thrive.

Imagine this scenario: that instead of fear, the students were confident to cast off the shame of what they had been doing because they knew that their parents would "pivot" to the expected response. That their parents would begin a dialogue with praise and laud their children's courage and strength to own such a struggle. That even before their parents delved into a discussion regarding the risks of such aggressive behavior, they knew that they would be met with love. Words formulated that reassured these students that, no matter how scarred or broken they were, they would unequivocally be loved.

Perhaps you might think that I am being too idealistic. Fair enough. I am not a birth parent. But, when I have student after student coming to me, their teacher, their principal, to tell me deep and very dark secrets about their lives, their thoughts, their feelings . . . something is clearly broken. The phone lines are dead, connection is lost, the signal is nowhere to be found.

How do you use your words to nurture your child?

As I said before, when my students criticize one another, say something snarky or mean-spirited, the English teacher in me makes them write. For every negative word uttered, they have to write twenty-five positive adjectives about that student. Sometimes they are irritated at this, so their word count increases because their attitude in dealing with the consequence is so poor. But 95 percent of the time, no matter how the assignment begins, it ends with the student quasi-enjoying the process. I can visibly see them get outside of themselves and focus on building up that particular classmate. And sometimes the words they pick have multiple meanings, and sometimes they use a couple of adjectives to kid and joke around. But always, at the end of the list, they sign and date the paper, and give it to their classmate with a sense of purpose. And for the person who is on the receiving end of the compliments, it is a fantastic moment—because we are creatures who crave attention. We want to know within our very core that we are good enough; that we are loved no matter what; that what we accomplish, no matter how great or minuscule, counts. Your child craves that positive reinforcement from you. They want nothing more than to know that who they are matters to you outside of anything else.

Every issue that your child faces should be important to you. You should be attuned to their needs—physical, mental, emotional. But you have to wake up. Be alert. En garde! It can't possibly be that your own life's dealings prevent you from noticing the Band-Aids going missing, the scissors nowhere to be found, the long sleeves and sweatshirts being worn four seasons round. It can't just be up to myself and my colleagues to be on top of the raging insecurities that your sons and daughters face and try to deal with in whatever ways possible. We have got to be a united front, you and I. I have your back and you have mine, and together—we have your child's.

Cutting is just the new trend of coping strategies among our youth. But

. . . WHEN I HAVE STUDENT AFTER STUDENT COMING TO ME, THEIR TEACHER, THEIR PRINCIPAL, TO TELL ME DEEP AND VERY DARK SECRETS ABOUT THEIR LIVES . . . SOMETHING IS CLEARLY BROKEN.

. . . EATING DISORDERS, RISKY SEX, DRUG AND ALCOHOL EXPERIMENTATION AND USE . . . IT'S ALL THE SAME: OUR CHILDREN ARE SCREAMING AT THE TOPS OF THEIR LUNGS FOR US TO LISTEN TO THEIR PLIGHTS. . . .

eating disorders, risky sex, drug and alcohol experimentation and use . . . it's all the same: Our children are screaming at the tops of their lungs for us to listen to their plights, to take notice of their stress, anxiety, and social failings. Why so often are their shrieks met with silence?

Part of my job in these moments is to not only take care of the child but to also then call in their parents to help them understand the circumstances. Some of these parents respond to the news with quick action. Shocked as they may be, they recognize their child's need for professional help. They take the news seriously, and they seek immediate action to partner with their student in learning how to cope with their feelings in positive and healthy ways. But others who look back at me with glassy stares; they are expressions of disconnect. Not disbelief so much as simply, "Huh. You don't say." One guardian told me that their student fell on a box of saws in their backyard, which was their rationale for the gaping wounds on the child's wrists. Another parent said to me, "Well, it makes sense. All of my kids have gone through something in middle school. I guess it was only a matter of time for [this student]." Still others have told me that it's everyone else's fault for somehow influencing their child's self-destruction.

Please, please, please don't be these parents. Don't settle for the "Oh, it's just a phase" routine—because often, it's just not. Your children are facing a mounting pile of stress and anxiety far greater than you ever knew in your formative years. The competition to be the best student and athlete, the thinnest and most beautiful, the highest achieving, and the smartest in the room, is at a climax of epic proportions. If we do not take a hard look at what this is doing to the self-esteem and self-worth of our youth, we will undoubtedly fail them, because we don't give to them the thing they need the most.

The thing far more valuable than any monetary contribution to their college fund, or new pair of headphones, or summer vacation in Hawaii—all of those things for which you strive will fade into the darkness of the inconsequential if you don't give your son or daughter the simplicity of a relationship with you. Healthy, supportive, loving, nurturing, 100 percent "I'm so proud of you." That is what makes the difference in a child's life. We as teachers see it every day—do you?

CHAPTER EIGHT
SAY "NO"

This might be the simplest chapter. Say "No."

It's very important that you tell your kids No.

It's not fair for you to make up for the time you aren't home with them, or simply don't feel like arguing, by giving into their every whim when you are, thereby leaving the rest of us to play the heavy.

No. It's such a simple yet powerful word.

"No, you cannot use your iPad before your homework is done, because it is important for you to grow in knowledge and wisdom."

"No, you can't watch that show, because its subject matter is way too mature for you."

"No, you can't use that language, because people make assumptions based upon how we speak."

Notice that each of my "no" examples is followed by a rationale. No one wants to be shut down without justification. Everyone wants reasoning behind someone else's directives toward them, and your kids are no different. From the beginning, explain to your kids the reasons for your family's rules and expectations. Involve your kids in the setting of parameters, incentives, goals, and restrictions. Let them know and feel that their ideas and opinions on family matters do in fact count. This will allow them to feel comfortable communicating with you about issues, both large and small, and it will certainly help them develop a healthy maturity and sense of autonomy.

I read the transcript of an interview with a renowned entrepreneur and fashion designer, describing her experiences in raising her two children. I was struck by one quote in particular: "I really explain things to them, because really, kids just want to be told the truth. They just do. They just want you to be truthful." Children are perceptive beings, and they can sense when we are lying, especially when it comes to rules and rationales. Be upfront with your kids. When you make a statement, be prepared to back it up. Be ready to explain to them why you are setting that boundary, and even ask them what they think about it. Asking them for their thoughts doesn't mean that you have to waffle about and change the mandate—but what it does do is allow your child to exercise their voice, feel validated that you care about their opinions, and it extends an olive branch of authenticity with your son or daughter. If they believe that you are honest with them, they will feel much more comfortable about being forthright with you.

Stop. Think. Act. This was one of my classroom themes. I put it up on my bulletin board with a giant traffic light, the colors red, yellow, and green indicating each step. Perhaps it's an image you want to relay to your own kids. Our children are impulsive—they do first and think later. Whether it's their high level of energy, lack of self-control, or simply childhood wonder, I cannot count the number of conversations I have had with one of my students after a poor decision:

Me: "What were you thinking?"

Student: "I wasn't."

Me: "Exactly. How can we change that?"

Usually, the student will respond with something to the effect that they could have slowed down; they could have not said or done what they did. I counter that with the reminder that they must think before doing. That even something as simple as pausing to take a breath, giving themselves two seconds to become present in the moment, those slight scratches on the surface of behavior modification can make all of the difference in the world when it comes to the end result in their course of action. But before I get to those scratches, I first need to tell them "No." No, what you are doing in this moment is not the right decision, and yes, we need to have a conversation about that.

To do this successfully, students need to be bombarded from all sides—from classroom to home to somewhere in between. You as parent and I as teacher must hold ourselves accountable to this same behavioral pattern if there is any hope for children to follow. To mold students into children who understand and respect boundaries and authority, you must raise your children to know the difference between right and wrong—for there is a difference. Teach them about the important qualities that make up sound character. If you rear your children to make choices with a foundation that is rooted in the basics of honesty, integrity, compassion, and wisdom, you will have no reason to judge their ability to make sound decisions. But all of this begins with saying "No."

In addition to the word *no*, I would also encourage the use of the word *consequence*. No one, and I mean no one, likes to be reminded that in life, there are always consequences. But the disservice we've done to this word is that we make it completely and totally, 100 percent buzzkill negative. But a consequence doesn't always have to be so bad. For example, a consequence of productivity at work is earning a bonus at the end of the quarter. A consequence of hitting two home runs at your company's softball game is that your team wins. A consequence of having a birthday is receiving presents and eating cake. A consequence of meeting your soul mate is falling in love.

See? Not all bad. But there are times when students need to understand that poor decision-making yields consequences to enable them to understand the gravity of strong choices.

Schools have always been known to be the enforcers of consequence. And while the trend has moved away from primarily the punitive to embrace, instead, the restorative, there are still drawn boundaries for students to understand the cause-and-effect outcomes of their choices. As an administrator, I seek to employ both. As noted previously, having students write positive adjectives for one another after negative talk is a restorative measure. A student putting together a presentation on recycling for younger students after littering the play yard would be another. There are many infractions for which this is a very effective approach. There are times, however, that warrant a more serious consequence.

I was riding in a taxi one evening, stuck in interminable Dallas traffic, and struck up a conversation with the driver. He was an immigrant from West Africa. A father of several older children in his home nation, he was now playing the role of stepfather to his wife's two children here in the United States. When he found out that I was a teacher, he simply shook his head. "The children are the ones running things now," he said. I chuckled, knowing what I know from my time in the classroom, but I was intrigued as to why he believed this to be true. He went on to describe the state of affairs regarding his stepsons, two boys who were becoming quite used to the inside of the principal's office. One was getting into fights, while the other was completely uninterested in anything school had to offer. Their apathy had grown to the point that they were suspended on more than one occasion. But he told me, the disappointment didn't end there.

Now you know the routine—student instigates a serious offense, student gets suspended, student is sent home . . . but, then what? The dual-working household can't simply come to a screeching halt when something like this occurs. Jobs are crucial—deadlines and deals need to be attended to. There are meetings, conference calls, people who depend on you as you depend on them. So when your child chooses to make a devastatingly poor decision, one that results in their suspension, the process is fairly simple: The disappointed parent frantically leaves work, goes to school to retrieve their child, takes them home, and then, through no fault of their own, heads back to the office. Because that is simply the reality. June Cleaver abandoned her post in the kitchen with an apron and cookie sheet and a day free to monitor the goings-on of her children a long time ago.

FROM THE BEGINNING, EXPLAIN TO YOUR KIDS THE REASONS FOR YOUR FAMILY'S RULES AND EXPECTATIONS. INVOLVE YOUR KIDS IN THE SETTING OF PARAMETERS, INCENTIVES, GOALS, AND RESTRICTIONS.

This is the exact scenario painted by my driving companion that day—the mother of the two children, working as a bus driver, went to the school, picked up her sons, dropped them off, and then headed back out to work. Dad had been at work at the time of the altercation and was stopping by home for a quick lunch before getting back on the road. He told me that he walked into the family room and saw one of his stepsons, happy as a clam, planted in front of the family computer watching porn. He said he was shocked—not by the porn-watching per se, as he was aware of adolescent curiosity. No, he was shocked by the complete and total lack of consequence for the boy's actions. "It's easier for him to get suspended than to stay in school. He gets to come home, play on the computer, and have no one telling him what to do," he said.

Neither he nor I were criticizing the dynamic of working parents, nor were we criticizing the school's decision to send this student home. I understood the dynamic of our conversation, instead, to reflect the need for at-school and at-home connections. The school rendered its consequence—removal from the learning and social environment. The question moves to: What's the at-home consequence? Shutting off the Wi-Fi? Taking away the student's access to technology? Bringing the student to work to understand the greater picture of why school is essential to their future? I have had parents cancel birthday parties, family vacations, and confiscate cell phones and laptops for months. One family, upon picking up their student after they brought a (unloaded) BB gun to school, immediately took their child to juvenile hall to show them the societal ramifications for poor decision-making.

Cause and effect. That is what we need our kids to grasp. You make a decision and something happens as a result. If your children, and my students, understand the power of "no," then they will understand the power of consequence—both positive and negative. But we both need to stress this. If I attempt to establish boundaries and rules and consequences in my classroom, I need to rely upon you, as parent, to establish those same basic principles at home. A lack of consistency leads to a lack of discretion, which leads to a plethora of negative consequences on the part of our youth. And to think this could be avoided altogether, or the impact at least lessened, if we just worked together.

As a principal, I have described our school's journey with several students as resembling the Greek myth about Sisyphus. Sisyphus was condemned to pushing a boulder up a hill only to watch it roll back down again when he was done. So, too, is the work that we as a faculty do with students who are not held to the same level of standards and expectations at home. Example: I am a stickler for the use of acceptable language.

But, how does that reinforcement stick if the same demands aren't being made once a student leaves my custody on campus? My words are absorbed onto Teflon at that point, and they slide right off because either:

> Mom, Dad, Grandma, or someone else won't make them speak in the same manner at home;

> or, their guardians don't care if their student gets in trouble in the first place;

> or, at least, doesn't let their involvement or communication on said indiscretion permeate outside of their familial interactions.

I had a student—well, one of many—who caught onto my game, if you will. They knew that from 8 a.m. to 3 p.m., they had to keep it together. I mean, they were teenagers, so I use "keeping it together" loosely. But they knew that once they stepped onto campus, they had to act a certain way. Once they were away from school grounds, however, that was a different story altogether: The floodgates were open, and they could let freedom ring. For one student in particular, it was riding his bicycle home each day without a helmet. He knew that when the wheels of his bike touched the campus, that helmet needed to be securely fastened. The same went for when the day was done. But after he was out of eagle-eyed supervision, the helmet was ditched completely. One day when the police pulled him and his helmetless head over for this serious infraction, the game suddenly permeated his outside-of-school life as much as it did during those eight hours inside.

Someone once said to me, "The hardest part of your job must be that no matter what you do during the day, it doesn't make a full impact if it's not being done at home, too."

As teachers, we come to realize that much of our work from 8 a.m. to 3 p.m. is unraveled the moment our students vacate campus. That boulder of molding, shaping, guiding, and coaching rolls right back down to the base of the proverbial hill the next morning, when said student comes bounding in the front doors of the school tossing expletives like confetti. And it doesn't just have to do with language. Healthy eating habits, time management, respect for self and others, responsible use of technology, self-advocacy, volunteerism, benevolence, tenacity, wearing a helmet—the list goes on and on. If we, as educators, aren't working in tandem with you, as parents, to establish similar expectations, then how can any of us expect to witness growth and change in your kids?

"No" cannot exist in a vacuum. "No" cannot be said once, brought to the bargaining table, and then somehow rationalized, or pulverized, into a tepid "Yes." No really does mean no. Sometimes you are able to give your child a choice—I often do the same thing. It's an easy way to establish clean boundaries, to steer your student in the proper direction, all the while giving them the opportunity to be involved in healthy decision-making.

"No, you can't avoid an assessment on *The Book Thief*, but you can choose which way you'd like to show me what you know: an essay or a quiz?"

"No, you can't throw your lunch away because it's essential that you fuel your body. But you can pick two of the three items to eat and take the rest home for a snack later."

"No, you can't go out without a jacket because it's too cold on your body. But you can pick between your parka and your fleece."

Explain. Elaborate. Establish. The three Es of productive conversation with your child. Will it always end in unicorns and harmony? Not a chance. But will it help to foster healthy conversation with your child? Absolutely.

Explain your rules, rationale, reasons.

Elaborate on your expectations when they push back.

Establish clear boundaries and expectations.

At the end of the day, we're all on the same road traveling to the same destination, as parents, teachers, and children. Let's be both clear and kind. Let's have boundaries. Let's travel together, holding one another accountable when our students want to assert their independence beyond the limits of what's acceptable.

CHAPTER NINE
WHO WORE IT BEST?

The recent shift from "free dress" to uniforms in our public schools is one that we should all be embracing. For the record, I am the product of Catholic schools, from first grade through high school, so uniforms were as natural to me as breathing. But for the student who is accustomed to selecting their own clothes and using said wardrobe as a means for self-expression, I can understand that the switch to a uniform would be shocking to say the least. But the benefits of students clad in the same garb day in and day out certainly outweigh the pitfalls. And even if your child's school has not yet adopted this growing trend, there are aspects of it to which every parent should be attuned.

I will preface this chapter by noting—the quantifiable data results on uniforms versus free dress are mixed. But the qualifiable data I have collected over the years has formed, for both myself and my inner circle of colleagues, a resounding "Yes" vote when it comes to a school's dress code.

Picture it:

> The student who fidgets with the perfect placement of the zipper on their hoodie throughout the entire duration of class only to end up taking it off completely come lunchtime.

> The child who pops their baseball cap forward and backward, off then back on again, over and over and over, never landing on just the right placement.

> The overwhelming concern if bracelets are stacked properly, or scrunchies, or any other accessory.

> The stress that comes from a scuff on a new pair of sneakers, or the hotbed of jealousy that arises around brands, styles, and logos.

You've heard it time and time again: Uniforms level the playing field. But from this teacher's perspective, I can assure you that the rumors are indeed true. Students who are dressed in the same clothes are more focused on school and far less distracted throughout the day. Teaching in a private school, my colleagues and I could set our watches to the chaos that would undoubtedly ensue on the last Friday of each month when the students were privileged with free dress.

The energy level on those days was far more palpable than on the days of uniformed plaid skirts and navy shorts. Kids would come bounding onto the play yard throwing far more caution to the wind as they ran and jumped and screamed, both with and at one another. Side-eyed glances from groups of girls who looked one another up and down before determining the success of each other's ensembles. And when it came time to line up for morning announcements, let's just say that the day generally got off to a late start as corralling the free-dressed masses took longer than usual.

Oh, and on those days, there was certainly less learning, too.

I will admit, once students grow accustomed to free dress, the calmer the learning environment will become. But the distraction that clothes cause is a long-lingering effect. Brands, labels, and Lululemon are a surefire way to separate the crowd.

I have watched the hierarchy of the middle school jungle unfold over something as inconsequential as yoga pants. And I am sorry, but there is nothing OK about that.

There was once a great divide in my class over athleisure wear. On a free-dress day, I overheard one girl say to another, "I only wear Lululemon. Doesn't everyone?" Without skipping a beat, another classmate within earshot of this conversation glanced down at her own clothes and said, "My pants came from Target. And I really don't care that much about it." I am not sure if I have ever been so proud of a student before. I jumped into the dialogue and gave immediate credit to the student who refused to kowtow to her peer's postulation.

Don't let your children get swept up in the current of inadequacies. Don't enable them to miss out on interacting with and knowing people of great worth and value even if their clothes tend to say otherwise.

Uniforms, or the requirement of a dress code, are also great ways to help your child understand the importance of sustainability. According to Vox, "Apparel and footwear production currently accounts for 8.1 percent of global greenhouse gas emissions, or as much as the total climate impact of the entire European Union." So whether you want to emphasize the value of a dollar, or the environmental impact of purchasing less clothing, stricter dress codes or uniforms altogether are incredible, tangible examples of how your child can learn to live without.

A seventh-grade student was complaining to me one day. It was a free-dress day, and she noted that when she went into her room to find something to wear, she didn't have much. Her mom was there and quickly jumped into the conversation. "You have clothes. You wear a uniform. That's not having nothing to wear. That's having exactly what you need to wear to be the best student you can be."

Go Mom!

I had a student who never wore a jacket. Never. Rarely did he even wear a sweatshirt. In the rain, nothing. In the freezing cold, nothing. He would ride his bicycle to and from school every day this way, no matter what the conditions. And his sibling did the same.

I have often wondered why so many of my students are reluctant to wear a jacket. Perhaps it is that they simply refuse. I know that, as a teacher, I have had many kids roll their eyes and throw a fit at the very suggestion of it. Perhaps, though, it is for financial reasons, which should always serve as a rallying cry for the collective school community to come alongside and help any family that is struggling. Perhaps, too, it's something else entirely. I don't know.

One thing I do know is that kids generally hate anything cumbersome. They are so eager to take off those bunchy, bulky jackets! Please, please—label your child's outwear! I cannot count the number of times I have helped a student or their parent deep dive into the Lost and Found bin looking for a missing jacket that was abandoned on the play yard. The number of frustrated emails I have received wondering about the location of a child's school sweater. In most of these cases, the items in question had no indication of to whom they belonged. You can order iron-on labels online, or simply use a Sharpie to write a student's name on the jacket's tag. But please don't send them to school in an article of clothing that can be lost, misplaced, or sent to purgatory in the Lost and Found bin without some sort of name marking.

Unfortunately, kids judge kids. I wish that that wasn't the reality, but I witness this every day. The recent shift in all schools—both private and public—to move toward uniform adoption versus free dress marks an attempt to level the playing field. If everyone wears the same thing, it enables students to prioritize school as the place for which it was intended—academia—instead of the proverbial catwalk. If all students don the same shorts, skirts, shirts, and sweats, then the disconnect between student A and student B diminishes. Never mind the added pressure of avoiding gang conflict due to clashing hues. In the case of clothes, keep it simple.

In the words of American environmentalist Donella Meadows: "We don't need bigger cars or fancier clothes. We need self-respect, identity, community, love, variety, beauty, challenge and a purpose in living that is greater than material accumulation."

TIPS FOR THE MORNING ROUTINE

Maximizing the time your child spends in the classroom is crucial— oftentimes, school schedules are created to give the most crucial subjects (i.e. phonics, reading, math) first thing in the morning when students' minds are fresh and supple for academic absorption.

Here are some tips for speeding up the morning routine (with or without uniforms) to get to school on-time and ready to learn:

Lay out clothes the night before—socks, undergarments, shoes—the works! This will prevent morning meltdowns over choosing what to wear in a frenzy.	Set a timer in the morning for various routines (i.e., showering, brushing teeth, eating breakfast, etc.). There are great timers out there, via apps, that help students visualize the time counting down with images of disappearing rubber ducks, pizza slices, and pirate ships.	Make sure that backpacks are packed the night before with homework and necessary supplies housed where they can be easily located. And, be sure that snacks and lunches are prepared ahead of time, too.	Have a week's end incentive for five days of on-time arrivals. A family movie night, pizza dinner, or extra time on iPad/ gaming device, etc. are all great ways to encourage everyone to get out the door efficiently.

CHAPTER TEN
PULL BACK THE CURTAIN . . .

You might remember your own teen years, when you agonized about your body changing. Maybe you worried about wearing a bikini in the summer, or you obsessed about doing push-ups to tighten your abs.

Your kids today are flooded by photos on social media sites like Instagram, Snapchat, and other messaging apps. They're getting a constant stream of bodies all day, and not just from celebrities. Your kids' friends are posting pictures of themselves and one another for everyone to look at and comment on.

So when a mother came to me to talk about how worried she was about her daughter's anxiety about her body image, I wanted to help. This mom told me how her young daughter was wearing a sweatshirt three sizes too big, in sweltering temperatures. This can often be a sign of body insecurity manifested in an eating disorder. If a child is hiding a significant weight loss, they will often conceal it beneath baggy clothing. But in this case it was just the opposite. The girl's body was developing, and clearly, she was trying to hide that fact. The struggle for Mom came when she tried to talk to her daughter about it, and her child refused to engage on the topic. She felt lost and didn't know what to do or whom to talk to.

Your child's body is going to change, just as this student's was. It is scary, terrifying, even earth-shattering for our children. As a seventh-grade teacher, my heart used to break for my students when they panicked over their first zit or cried when their period came out of nowhere. I'd actually venture to say that puberty is one of the hardest times of life—to watch your body morph and expand without any sense of control.

Around this topic and beyond, both the media and their peers will leave an impression on every kid, shaping their ideology about what makes them popular, happy, attractive, whole . . . or just the opposite. Run a basic search of Instagram body influencers, and you are sure to find a cache of negativity affecting both girls and boys—accounts like @top_skinny_girls and the hashtags #skinnyfat, #skinnyboy, and #starvebitch, all of which espouse extreme measures to achieve unrealistic beauty ideals while promoting body shaming and insecurity.

So, I ask you—in a world where Snapchat and Instagram feeds receive the bulk of both your attention as well as your child's, has body positivity, doled out from behind the high-gloss resolution of a smartphone, actually made us feel worse about ourselves?

DON'T JAM TO YOUR KIDS'
MUSIC—THEY DON'T LIKE IT.
DON'T SPEAK THEIR
JARGON—YOU . . . HAVE NO
CLUE WHAT IT IS YOU ARE
ACTUALLY SAYING.

Your child clicks "like," swipes right, comments, and expresses their support through cartoon high fives and candy-colored hearts. Accepting the invitations of total strangers, they follow those on social media who appear to empower them through images of toned muscles, jutting hipbones, and real talk about cutting carbs, and that it's what's on the outide that counts. How does the impact of these virtual influencers extend into their real lives? How can we help them find a way to take the wit, wisdom, and know-how of these dynamic experts and apply their recommendations to our kids' day-to-day routines, discerning, of course, who is in possession of the experiential chops to be giving them advice in the first place?

Well, first—they have to stop posting and start moving. Start moving in the direction of filling their feeds with posts, images, and messages that build themselves up, not make them feel bad about themselves or more insecure than their boisterous inner critics seek to. Move away from following those influencers who perpetuate the promotion of unhealthy body goals and leave our children feeling guilty and inadequate.

Instead, let's help them move toward finding the influencers who exist for the very purpose of influencing them to celebrate their strength, their confidence. Who inspire them to change their habits, learn a new skill, relate to the struggle of others, or become better, more empathetic versions of themselves. But it's not enough for your child to just read these posts or watch their stories or follow their YouTube channels—no, kids need to absorb what these digital personas have to teach them and get moving towards a physically, emotionally, socially whole version of themselves.

So, back to my mother-daughter dilemma. I first recommended that they go shopping together. "Make it a fun day," I said. "Let your daughter pick out a sports bra that feels comfortable to her. Don't force a particular style on her, but rather, let her feel that sense of control."

See, if you allow your child to assume the driver's seat in scenarios when they are protected on all sides and shrouded in security, you will not only help them exercise sound decision-making skills, but you will also help them find healthy ways to practice choice and self-advocacy—two vital skills as they grow into independent individuals.

I also advised her to find ways to share her own personal experiences with her daughter. "Don't use your memories to minimize her current anxiety," I said. "But instead, let her know that, even though life might seem a bit wonky right now, even scary, she's still the same awesome person she always was."

Fill in a funny anecdote about your adolescent experience—we all have them.

Self-deprecation as a means of establishing trust and connection with your child when they themselves are struggling with some of those same loathing feelings can really bolster your relationship.

Even I myself can speak to the power that this connection resonates.

For example, to this very day, I remember being a kid when my friend's mom told us about a time when she was in middle school and her tampon string was hanging outside of her bathing suit at a classmate's birthday party. She told us that it was humiliating and mortifying, but she survived. She empathized with our struggle by illustrating her own embarrassment. Moments like this worked then, and they work now.

Pull back the curtain. . . . It's easier said than done. Thanks to today's social and online media, it's not easy to compare your childhood to your child's. Yet the situations, scenarios, moments, and experiences from your childhood haven't changed very much. You can remember and recognize what your own kid is going through.

Let's take that first school dance, for instance. Remember that? I've taught many seventh graders who experienced their first dance ever.

Yes, those pivotal two and one half hours of supreme awkwardness when the boys and girls retreat to the farthest corners of a dark and dank school gymnasium. . . .

The girls show up in outfits that are overcoordinated, overaccessorized, and overdone. Some of them appear to be wearing costumes, not clothes. The boys show up sweaty and clammy, and they pace nervously back and forth, not quite sure how to actually dance.

A DJ blasts pop music in all its glory while parent chaperones sway their hips from one side to the other. Yes, they think to themselves, I've so got this.

Let me be the one to break it to you: Trying out some cool moves at your kid's dance will not help them. I realize this sounds harsh, but the more you try to be the "cool parent," the less cool you are.

>Don't jam to your kids' music—they don't like it.

>Don't speak their jargon—you are not Urban Dictionary and have no clue what you are actually saying.

>Be comfortable in your role as the mentor, guide, sage. The most successful parents embrace that very title—parent. Not friend. Not peer. Parent.

One Monday morning, my students were worked up and anxious after their first dance. When I asked them what was wrong, they proceeded to tell me that one of their chaperones was taking pictures of them during the dance and texting those snaps to other parents in the class. This parent even went as far as to tell the kids that these photos would be put in the school's yearbook. They were embarrassed and humiliated. They couldn't understand why a classmate's parent would want to do that to them. Some even told me that they weren't going to go to any more dances because their own parents had teased them so much when they got home, it just wasn't worth the trauma.

I don't blame them. Of course, given that their classmate was one of my students, I couldn't verbalize my true shock and dismay at what they had been subjected to—that wouldn't have been fair, for it wasn't that student's fault. But on the part of their guardian, it wasn't right, fair, or OK in any regard. These are formative years of social interactions and development. These mixers, dances, and coed birthday parties are moments that lay a foundation for how your child will relate to their peers and members of the opposite sex for years to come. How many times do we chuckle at an illustration of the poor sack lying on a psychiatrist's couch, wailing on about how they were so misunderstood as a child. That their parents had embarrassed them beyond repair. Don't be the reason for that bill.

Hopefully you didn't have children because you were lonely or lacking in friends. It is absolutely fine to cultivate a healthy "friendship" with your children—one of fun, camaraderie, laughter, and shared interests. Take selfies—minus the duck lips. Play their music—but explain to them the reason that you choose the clean versions. (You do download the clean versions, right? More on that later.) That is what creates sound dynamics and successful parent-child relationships. But remember that your child craves structure and rules and boundaries. They probably can't verbalize this to you, but it is essential to their development that you do in fact set parameters.

I have found that this is a critical area of conflict between teacher and parent. At school, the teacher seeks to abide by the guiding rules of the institution and expects the same from their scholars. Meanwhile at home is the parent who is able to spend less and less time with their children, often through no fault of their own. It's just how life is. So how does that parent deal with their guilt? They give into every whim of their child, either simply out of shame for the fact that their schedule doesn't allow for more one-on-one time and interaction with their kids, or they just don't want to be labeled as "mean" or "strict." And while in the moment it seems like the perfect remedy, the ideal Band-Aid, in the long run your child will be worse for wear. The child without consistent parameters doesn't simply wake up one day and know the rules for social etiquette, the

WE NEED TO MODEL WAYS
FOR KIDS TO BOTH ASK FOR
AND RECEIVE HELP. WE NEED
TO GIVE KIDS THE TOOLS
AND TECHNIQUES TO
PROBLEM-SOLVE ON THEIR
OWN WHEN WE AREN'T
THERE.

boundaries of law and order; no, the child without consistent parameters is the adult who parties far too hard, breaks the law too many times, hurts others too often and too much. I'm not overexaggerating here—you have to understand that every teachable moment you let slip by because you are feeling bad about your sporadic presence during your child's life are the moments when you fail them the most.

Likewise, some parents take boundaries to such an extreme they're denying their children the experience to learn and grow on their own. I'm talking about "helicopter parents," the ones who are constantly putting down new boundaries. As in, letting a child play only in the backyard because it's fenced. Or going on a hike as long as you're holding your kid's hand the whole time. Or letting your kid go on a school field trip only if Mom is there.

"I feel sorry for kids today," a Lyft driver recently told me as we crawled through rush hour traffic downtown, after I told him that I was a school principal.

I certainly know why I feel this way, but I was curious as to what prompted him to tell me this. He said he was a father to a son who was now in college.

He recalled having a group of his son's friends over to a swim party when they were just scratching the surface of their elementary school years. One of the boys soiled his swim trunks, so my Lyft comrade got him new clothes to change into. The child rebounded from his accident immediately and went on to play with the other kids both on the grass and in the pool. When the boy's mother arrived, according to him, she "flipped out." "Why?" I asked. Well, A) she didn't want him wearing the clothes of any other children (hello, gratitude?); and, B) she was even more upset by the fact that he was playing in the grass. His hands were dirty. She paid no mind to the fact that he was laughing, and running, and playing—being a kid! She immediately scooped him up off of the grass, wiped off his hands with an antibacterial towelette, and took him home.

Oh, and the driver never saw those swim trunks again.

Was she always going to be there to wipe his hands, he questioned. Would she teach him about the importance of showing gratitude for the benevolence of others over her need for him to be pristine at all times? Would this child ever be able to understand the difference between the glorious innocence of being a child versus the rigidity of his mom's expectations? I guess we'll never know.

A stickler for cleanliness myself, I certainly won't be hypocritical enough to criticize this mom's concerns over the messy—Purell and Clorox Wipes have always had a home in my classroom! But I do believe that his tale speaks to the heart of raising a well-adjusted child.

We need to model ways for kids to both ask for and receive help.

We need to give kids the tools and techniques to problem-solve on their own when we aren't there.

You, as the parent, have the power to put up boundaries and safeguards to protect your kids from the world—including the online world. It's OK to be the heavy. It's OK if your kids don't like you today. You are your child's guide, sage, mentor, coach, confidant, and protector. Parent first, friend later.

And please remember to teach your kids to say "thank you" when someone rescues them from a pair of soiled swim trunks.

YOU, AS THE PARENT, HAVE THE POWER TO PUT UP BOUNDARIES AND SAFEGUARDS TO PROTECT YOUR KIDS FROM THE WORLD—INCLUDING THE ONLINE WORLD.

CHAPTER ELEVEN
BORING IS THE NEW BLACK

Sometimes life is boring. Unabashedly, unequivocally, undeniably B-O-R-I-N-G. All of the time? No. But at certain times? Yes.

Because for us to establish a successful village as parents and teachers, we must raise children who understand that there's a balance, an ebb and flow to life that sometimes climaxes in the most exciting of endings; but that sometimes, even most of the time, life is stagnant, dull, and dare I repeat it . . . boring. In a culture and climate of 24/7 instant gratification, it is difficult for today's kids to grasp that the world is not always going to cater to their every whim, entertaining them with a nonstop barrage of action and excitement, each moment louder, bigger, and bolder than the one before it. Nope. Sometimes, life is just plain boring.

It was my first wedding anniversary, and my husband and I left in mid-November to celebrate for the better part of two weeks. In anticipation of my absence, I prepared a very well-developed and cohesive lesson plan for the substitute to implement. It was a blend of assignments and activities that would continue to mold my students' comprehension and fulfill several requirements of grade-level standards, but it was simple in nature so that any substitute could execute it with ease. Approximately three days into my absence, my colleague reported to me that one of my students said that the English class was "boring." I believe it went something to the effect of:

Sub: "Please take out last night's homework to correct."

Student: "This is so boring!"

Excuse me? Since when was the class asked what they thought of the lesson plan in the first place? Don't get me wrong, every student should have a voice and feel empowered to develop their opinions and communicate said feelings in appropriate ways. But when your son or daughter is so used to being "entertained" that they cannot fathom the very idea of sitting for a few minutes and developing the tactile skills of writing and the modalities of listening and reading, well, then we have a problem. I won't even begin to address the overriding issue of a lack of respect and self-control in the face of frustration. Let's just look at the language this student chose to utter: "This is so boring!" If you do not raise your children to understand that each experience that they face is a moment for them to grow and refine themselves as learners, givers, and all-around decent human beings, you are part of perpetuating the all-about-me pandemic we face.

Maybe this student was in a bad mood. Perhaps they were overtired, not feeling tip-top. I sympathize. We all have those days.

As your son or daughter wakes up and heads out the door to school, I encourage you to remind them that they are on their way to work—to a job, if you will.

"Today, we both have work that we need to accomplish at our jobs. My boss expects me to do my best. What do your teachers expect from you?"

"What is one significant thing that you can accomplish today at school?"

"What can you do today to earn your best paycheck at the end of the quarter?"

Paying attention in class, engaging in discussion, producing classwork and homework and test scores that speak to their intellect as a capable human being—this is their career for now. And their report card? That's their paycheck. Some of my favorite moments of parent-student collaboration have involved this very analogy, and almost every time, it lands with students because it is a tangible, relatable concept that puts everyone on the same level.

No job is cotton candy, acrobats, and dancing clowns each day. Call me crazy, but I think we all would love to show up at work and play video games, inhale copious amounts of junk food, and surf YouTube for eight hours. But the reality is that your daily grind, my daily grind, is less than stimulating over half of the time. Chances are that, like me, you learned a long time ago that while life may be your oyster, it certainly doesn't jump out of its shell, crack a few jokes, and spoon itself into your mouth.

I was speaking with a friend who's the mother of two, and her youngest had just started kindergarten. She was a newly single parent at the time, and our conversations often moved from Pilates and shopping to dialogue about her kids, knowing that I was an educator. One day, she was describing an encounter with her daughter in which the girl wanted to leave the dinner table although her brother was still eating his meal. My friend told her daughter that she needed to remain at the table until everyone was done with their food. The daughter countered her mother's request: "What am I supposed to do? Can I draw? Can I go watch TV? This is boring."

Now, my friend is what I like to call "old school." She firmly believes in teaching her children the basics of good behavior—respecting others, telling the truth, communicating with authenticity (yes, she actually demands this of her young children). So she remained firm. "No, you can't leave the table until everyone has finished their meal. But we can talk and plan what we should all do together once dinner is done."

After telling me this story, she and I agreed that boredom IS when true creativity abounds. Only in boredom do we create and imagine. And seeing that this holds true for adults, begin to conceptualize what your children's young, formative, active minds could and would conjure up if you simply allowed them to be bored every once in a while.

I'll say it again: Let your children be bored. Set aside time when you do not plan anything—no playdates, no sports, or practices, or lessons. No iPad, tablet, phone, or laptop. Give them time to simply be. And then, after they grow bored with complaining that they are bored, watch your kids.

Simply sit back and see what unfolds. Perhaps it will be a scrap of paper that attracts their attention. Maybe a pencil will magically turn into an artist's instrument. Maybe they will resort to hanging out with their little brother or sister. Maybe their bed will finally be made because they have nothing else better to do than contribute to the betterment of the household. Unless they are playing with matches or juggling knives, be excited. Watching what your children put their minds to when they are not being bombarded by a thousand signals and transmissions is fantastic.

I understand what a challenge this can be for Type A parents! The very idea of letting your children run hog wild trying to self-soothe themselves out of their boredom is a little too loosey-goosey for your taste. No problem. I get it. Believe me, there are times in the classroom when even the most flaccid of teachers grows impatient with the chaos that comes from "free time." So be prepared. Have an area of your house stocked with supplies for these very moments. Allow your students to experience the important lesson of being bored—but do it on your own terms. Fill a cupboard with art supplies. In the kitchen, make sure your kids can find the ingredients to make cookies or brownies. Make a list of household needs that are pending completion, perhaps even with an extrinsic reward attached for whoever accomplishes a project. Go ahead and be prepared for boredom. Schedule it on the calendar if you want! Just so long as your children's creativity, spontaneity, and appreciation for moments of self-direction are nurtured and encouraged. These moments will fuel them for success both in and outside of the classroom walls.

BOREDOM IS WHEN TRUE
CREATIVITY ABOUNDS. ONLY
IN BOREDOM DO WE CREATE
AND IMAGINE.

CHAPTER TWELVE
SOMETHING TO BELIEVE IN

My classroom used to be haunted. Yes, that's what I said—haunted.

Now, I know what you're thinking—that sounds certifiably nuts. Perhaps. But, I am in fact serious. Maybe this idea resonates with you: the notion of a spirit from some other realm walking amongst us to send a covert message, handle some unfinished business. But, maybe too, nothing would ever seem more far-fetched than this claim. Fair enough. But, in my case, it's true.

Legend has it that my ghost was my predecessor. A nun, actually, who didn't want to give up her profession as an educator when it came time to retire. She fought tooth and nail to stay on, but she was overruled. Outrun. But despite the adversity, she was determined to never stop being a part of the seventh grade. So, long after she passed away, she would pop by every now and then to make sure things were running smoothly. I nicknamed her Sister Mary Clarence, in honor of the greatest nun herself, Whoopi Goldberg. The funny thing was that when my class was under control, my room was tidy, and things were progressing at a stable clip, she was nowhere to be found. But, when things became wonky, or I was gifted a more rambunctious class than others, she made her existence known and with frequency.

Now, that's a dedicated teacher.

The whys and hows of my students and I knowing the presence of this spirit doesn't matter (though, if you pressed me further, I would tell you that my clock spun backwards, the door to our classroom opened and closed on its own, and the phone even rang when unplugged from the wall). The important thing is that we believed in this spirit—my students and I. We were united around a common idea that, year after year, connected us all.

What does your child believe in?

According to therapist Angela Komisar in an OpEd for *The Wall Street Journal:* "Today, the U.S. is a competitive, scary, and stressful place that idealizes perfection-ism, materialism, selfishness, and virtual rather than real human connection. . . . Spiritual belief and practice reinforce collective kindness, empathy, gratitude, and real connection."

As a middle school teacher, I would tell my students, with frequency, about the necessity that their development as humans be rooted in the belief in something bigger than them. God, Mother Nature, Charles Darwin, even our own Sister Mary Clarence.

Think back to when you were in middle school, high school even. You wanted the world to think you were invincible. That you could do no wrong. That the universe revolved around you. You were twelve, maybe thirteen years old, and you knew it all. Once you crossed the threshold of using deodorant or began to understand the laws of attraction, you assumed that you had it all figured out. Sure, you might have been insecure about the breakout of pimples across your t-zone; might have been wracked with panic, thinking that you blew it with your crush by taking a tumble during gym class; might have replayed a lunchtime conversation over and over in your mind, obsessing about what you said and if it was funny enough. But, would you ever dare to vocalize it? Not. A. Chance.

So, in the process of stuffing down all those feelings of insecurity, you created, instead, a false sense of superiority and dominance, purporting yourself king or queen of the social castle.

It's known as adolescent egocentrism, which is characterized by a belief that the world rotates solely around you, often resulting in an inflated confidence, intense jealousy of others, or supreme isolation. Adolescent egocentrism was a theory founded by psychologist Dr. David Elkind. According to Corrina Horne of betterhelp.com, "Dr. Elkind studied adolescents ranging from 11–18 years old, focusing on how they perceived the world compared to their adult counter-parts. Dr. Elkind discovered that teenagers were largely unable to differentiate between their own perceptions and the perceptions of others. Teenagers consis-tently believe their view is the only possible view, and all other ideas are false or entirely nonexistent."

And, as a result, students go boldly into the good night puffed up with bravado and oozing superiority. I have seen it more times than I can count. The student who begins posting scandalous selfies on Snapchat. The kid who no longer has any interest in following the rules of basic common courtesy. The child who begins to utter expletives and jargon that causes their parents' heads to explode. Humility goes out the door and in comes an ego that overflows that adolescent well of insecurity. And, in most of the cases that I observed as a teacher, none of these students believed in much.

When I taught, I was in a parochial school, which made the "believe in some-thing bigger than yourself" conversation a bit simpler as faith formation was part of our curriculum. But even with students in other schools or in conversations with friends of mine who are parents, I have noted that in a world that is becoming increasingly insular—one in which we all seek to be the expert, the perfectionist, the influencer, the oracle with all the answers—if we have any hope of establishing some sense of humility within our children, then they need to believe that they are part of a much greater puzzle.

Some students challenge the faith in which they were raised. Others seek to study new forms of religion or worship. Some find their footing in the belief that they will one day be the next LeBron James or Andy Warhol. Still others study the stars and dabble in astrology. But, for students who grow up without aligning themselves with an appreciation for the sheer mass of the heavens or universe, the development of their sense of self and place in the world will be both jaded and off-kilter.

I once polled my class of twenty or so eighth-grade students to learn what they imagined for their futures. What were their hopes and dreams? The ambitions they cultivated and the goals to which they aspired. More than half the class couldn't say. They had no scope of envisioning what lay ahead for them. I was heartbroken. How could they have no idea how to map out what they wanted for their future? You see, if our kids don't believe that their possibilities are vast, their potential endless, their fate a collection of universal happenstances all leading to awesome results, then they are blind to what's out there. Any confidence they seek to muster is muddied and unfounded without a foundation of belief.

So, what's the solution?

Talk to your child: Ask children for their opinions; discover what they envision for their futures. Are they active participants in your family's faith traditions? If not, then give them the space to tell you why—without judgment or reproach. From there, find out what they do believe in. And, if they don't know—join them on a journey of discovering what that might look like.

Place emphasis on non-judgment: It is both normal and natural to envelope your child in your family's beliefs and traditions in their early and formative years. But, as your child matures and grows into his or her own thoughts and ideas, it is equally normal for their belief system to evolve. Create space for their autonomous self-discovery.

Model your own beliefs: Kids hate hypocrisy, so be acutely aware that you are modeling to them that which you espouse. If your faith is in prayer—pray. If your faith is in nature—make recycling and caring for the outdoors apparent. If your faith is in humanity—display random acts of kindness and compassion to all people. Live it, walk it, exemplify it.

As your child grows, you will undoubtedly go through times of feeling both connected to and disconnected from them. But, much like my students and I were bonded by the belief in dear Sister Mary Clarence, so, too, can you find unification with your child through a foundation of faith, hope, and the conviction that there is so much more out there for them to explore.

CHAPTER THIRTEEN
FRIEND REQUEST

At the start of my first year as a teacher, several moms asked me out to dinner. Being a naïve rookie, I gladly accepted their invitation. They chatted about my background, inquired if I was dating, and "filled me in" on the what's what and who's who of the class. It was great—we bonded; we were suddenly all on the same team.

Or . . . were we?

As the year progressed and the class became their rowdy, pre-pubescent selves, I was required to enforce discipline. Granted, I was a brand-new teacher, so it was a bumpier ride than other years on record. Nevertheless, as I've said, consequences should be and were given out equitably and universally, no matter whose son or daughter was responsible for the chaos.

But what about my new group of mom friends? They expected that their children would be above the law; after all, we were girlfriends now.

This is when I realized a hard lesson: As a teacher, I am not your friend. Teachers are not buddies you take out for drinks, or with whom you gossip about your personal life or the personal lives of other families in the school. Teachers need boundaries to teach, and parents need to respect this. I didn't cave; I stood my ground, knowing that at the end of the day, I was conducting myself as the professional my craft demanded of me.

As a teacher, it is not my job to have fun with the parents of my students. It is not my job to be best friends with the moms and, dare I say, dads in my class from year to year. Sure, I absolutely am and should be cordial, collaborative, and communicative, but my primary responsibility is to be the best teacher possible for their children. And no amount of girl talk and skinny margs can or should affect that.

I have worked in institutions where fundraisers and evening events occur, and after my first year of teaching, I decided to never attend one particular event again. Teachers should not be expected to show up at social functions where alcohol is flowing and conversations grow out of hand. I have watched dads flirting with other moms, and those same moms grinding on the dance floor against men who were clearly not their partners. I have seen parents become far too inebriated and begin conversations with myself and other staff members that they wouldn't dream of discussing if not for the effects of their night out.

Fights in the parking lot; hooking up behind the gymnasium. I've seen it all.

Several years later, when I was asked why I wasn't attending that year's event, I was blunt. I told the chairperson that I felt uncomfortable being put in a position of socializing with the school's parents. I described to her my feelings about being caught in a situation which could indefinitely affect my impartiality. Surprisingly enough, she got it. She understood from where I was coming—she even went beyond validation to something along the lines of, "You have a life outside of school, too. I get that. Your free time should be just that—free."

So please, don't friend your child's teacher on Facebook or slide into their DMs. Don't come into the classroom on Monday morning before school trying to hash out last weekend's party.

You have your life, and the teacher has theirs. Let it exist in the balance and harmony for which it was intended. I promise you that in the end, this is better for you, your kids, and dare I say it, even better for the teacher.

CHAPTER FOURTEEN
YES, VIRGINIA, THERE ARE LOSERS

As a teacher, I did my best to treat students equally. Whether I was answering questions, doling out consequences, or grading essays, I aimed to treat every encounter with an equal approach. As an administrator, I believe it crucial to collaborate with my teaching staff on this topic—often and with purpose.

In a class of twenty-five, thirty, sometimes thirty-five kids, I find it essential to make certain that all students feel respected, acknowledged, supported when they fail, and commended when they succeed. The measure of success differs, of course, from student to student. For some students, success is measured in the grade of A, while others find success in Cs. Neither is better nor worse than the other—it is all simply based upon the achievement threshold for that individual.

But despite every attempt at equity that my colleagues and I can muster, at the end of the day, the truth remains: There are winners and there are losers. This means that there will always be someone who achieves higher on a test, scores a home run in a recess game of kickball, wins the Perfect Attendance award. It doesn't mean that the student who stayed home with strep throat "lost" or the B+ scored on last week's math quiz didn't "win." But you can't escape it. Someone will always come out on top, and someone will always fall slightly behind. It is just the way life works.

I have had students who practically ran themselves into the ground seeking so hard to be on top academically. They burned the midnight oil studying, researching, revising, and rewriting. They sent me emails at midnight wondering about an assignment's minutiae and burst into tears if they missed a single problem on their test.

Other students have tried so hard to perfect their appearance. They asked to leave class three times within an hour to check out their reflection in the bathroom mirror, skipped lunch to make sure that they kept their calories down, and immediately started the rumor mill the moment anyone else appeared to be diminishing their physical edge.

There was the athlete who threw a fit on the basketball court when they, or a teammate, blew a shot. The candidate for student council election who smack talked their competition and ripped down their posters.

No one wants to come in second.

You see, our kids are acutely aware that there will always be another individual who is deemed smarter, faster, prettier, thinner, richer, bolder, louder, wiser. . . . It doesn't stop once they leave adolescence, nor is it going to anytime soon. For centuries, we have had to embrace this fact. We may not like it, but it remains to this day a fact of life.

Yet I, as a teacher, have found that in the myriad of ways academics has morphed over the years, one of the paramount changes is that we seek to placate and pander to feelings over reality. What we want to see or to be true versus the quantifiable data in front of us.

For example, when a parent used to sign their children up for Little League, or basketball, or gymnastics, they took upon themselves the understanding that their child may not always be on the winning side of the sport. There might have been games, even seasons, when their child's team was the underdog, the underscored, the underachiever. But they knew that these moments of being second-best were opportunities for character building, resilience—chances to allow their sons and daughters moments for bolstering conviction, motivation, and endurance in even the most frustrating of circumstances. No one ever sought for their children to fail—but the vast parent majority used to realize that only when you are on the bottom can you truly appreciate the view from the top.

Take this scenario: Your child has an exceptionally strong quarter in school. They earn straight As. That, on its own, is the sole accomplishment—they proved their academic prowess by achieving what can only be described as a perfect report card. But I ask you—is that enough? Are you able to use that as the ultimate showcase of their success? Or does there have to be more? Does their motivation become diminished if they also don't receive schoolwide recognition with a certificate and a pin and the fanfare and applause of an audience?

What is the threshold we are willing to use as measure for a child's achievement? I'm afraid that we have evolved to a place where, unless praise is doled out in gold stars, marching bands, and $20 bills, a well-placed high five and "Congratulations" is no longer sufficient.

Intrinsic motivation has lost its value in a world where the extrinsic is all that we will allow to satisfy our starving egos.

We don't call games by their wins and losses anymore at school. No, instead we use phrases like "gave a great effort" or "tried their best"—which is fine. Believe me when I tell you how important positive reinforcement is for your kids' resolve and tenacity. High fives or an ice cream treat after school for a job well done are great strategies for communicating your pride in what your child has achieved. But along those same lines, if we are celebrating when our kids succeed, why do we prevent ourselves from also acknowledging when the other team, the other student, the other you-fill-in-the-blank here, simply had a better day? Why are we so afraid of straight talk? Yes, Virginia, there are losers.

Don't underestimate a child's resilience. Your child will get over their losses.

So many times I have had parents beating down my door to contest a bad grade or a consequence for poor choices made by their sons or daughters. And the funniest part of all is that while their child may have been bummed out for a moment, even a bit dejected, they got over it. So why can't we? Why is it so important that children be number one all the time? Were you? Far from it, I imagine; and the reality is, that is how life works. Some days, the scale's balance is in your favor, and other days, it gets counted as a loss. A loss.

In an article for *USA Today*, Sonja Haller explores this very topic, calling out the "lawn mower parent"; those who seek to "mow down all of children's challenges, discomforts, and struggles."

Hannah Hudson, the editorial director of weareteachers.com, elaborates: "The problem is not a parent's willingness to help a child succeed, that's admirable and understandable. The problem comes from a parent's repeated efforts to eliminate any and all struggle so that children are ill-equipped when they grow up and life inevitably goes sideways."

Duquesne University professor Karen Fancher narrates the impact of lawn-mowing parenting on a child's transition from youth to adolescent to college age and beyond:

> . . . as adults or just on the precipice of adulthood, these students have communication difficulties, lack a sense of personal motivation and believe they're not good enough to accomplish things on their own because lawn mower parents have cleared and charted paths and removed obstacles.

I was at a Thanksgiving dinner when a mother of two started chatting with me. She was recounting a story about her son's baseball team, and how in recent seasons, they weren't keeping score. The league and its parent majority felt that keeping score was too hurtful for the kids, making them feel bad about themselves. This parent was clearly in the minority, telling me how silly she thought these rules were. She went so far as to state that sheltering children from the fact that in life there will be winners and losers was doing a disservice to their development.

"Life keeps score," she said. "There are days when you are on the winning

DON'T UNDERESTIMATE
A CHILD'S RESILIENCE.
YOUR CHILD WILL GET OVER
THEIR LOSSES.

side of opportunities, relationships, job offers. But other days, we don't come out on top." She went on, "How will my kids be able to handle the low points of life if we don't start training them to deal with a loss now?"

What a relief to hear this mother's perspective! I wanted to hug her because kids need to learn how to use their "disappointment muscles." This is what will carry them through life when, say, a coworker gets a promotion and they do not. Or they get turned down after a job interview.

What about honors in college, or peers who earn more money than they do one day? What about the colleague with the hotter wife, the slimmer waistline, more hair, or a faster car? What then?

The lost games or the consequences at school that force your child to stay in from recess one day, those are the moments that shape their abilities to be rational and clear-thinking adults. The scars of a lousy basketball season when they are eight will fade. But the detriment to their future if you do not acknowledge that loss will remain for decades to come.

How do you avoid this? First and foremost, positive reinforcement should be a habit so routine, so ingrained in your relationship with your child that they know, no matter what the outcome, that they are wholly and completely loved. They don't always have to come out on top—they still have your unending support and encouragement to sustain them even in the rain.

Be aware—be very aware! Find small moments, little glimmers that maybe no one else saw. Perhaps your child didn't even realize it. But remark on those things. I have had students bring me work that is shoddy at best. And yes, I tell them that it is shoddy and did not receive the best of their effort or attention. But then I tell them something that I appreciated. A comment as simple as, "Wow! You really had a great sentence here!" Or "I really like where you were headed with this thought." These little "wins" will keep your child's motivation from being crushed in the face of defeat.

Next, have a conversation around what it means to lose; to come in second; to bomb a test or give the wrong answer. Dialogue on how to receive (and give) constructive criticism, and reiterate that often in life, they will not win. Every year in my graduation address to my students, whether as a teacher or a principal, I tell my students to fail. I give them permission to try and fall and try again. I know that they have the tenacity and know-how to be able to succeed eventually. But I also want them to prove to themselves that they can do it. When we seek to shroud our kids in Bubble Wrap, throw scorekeeping out the window, and give everyone in the room a trophy, we're not aptly preparing them for what's to come.

Here's another concern when kids are so worried about not coming out on top, and possibly disappointing not only themselves, but their parents: hurting themselves.

As a both a teacher and a principal, I have seen students undo the lining of their jackets to hide scissors or blades. I have seen students attempt to leave my classroom day after day, immediately after lunch, to purge their meals; students who dodge a lecture in order to drink vodka disguised as Gatorade in the bathroom. I have had more conversations than I can recount with students who feel that life is just too tough, and they want to end it all.

The problem with self-harm is complex and layered. I am no psychiatrist, nor do I claim to be one. But I am an observer; someone who has been witness to the downward spiral of many students simply because the expectations were too intense, the comparisons to other more accomplished peers or siblings too far out of reach.

Parents need to ask themselves, Do I want what is truly best for my child? Or do I seek to live vicariously through their accomplishments?

What is lacking in a parent's own life should not serve as a rationale for forcing their student to fill those very voids and inadequacies. That's not a child's job, and that's not how we, as a village, should rear them. No parent should sit by and watch their child slack off, falter, stray off course. But it is your job, in those moments of frustration when they do fall short or lack initiative, to also point out where they succeed, where they shine, where they seem to be their best selves. Maybe your child is really not academically minded—college is not for everyone. Maybe right now your son or daughter would much rather play video games with their Fortnite friends than kick around a soccer ball on their school's team. Sure, you may want them to play sports, or dance, or sing, or take trombone lessons. But do they? If your child is not focused on their academics, is withdrawing from interpersonal interactions and delving into a sedentary lifestyle, that most certainly requires prodding, and there are tools and techniques for coaxing them into hitting the books, inhaling fresh air, and embracing in-person dialogue a little bit harder. But everything else? Let it go. If your child wants to pursue modern dance, buy them a leotard. If they think that fly fishing is their life's ambition, pick up the rod and help them explore. Don't stand in your child's way just because you secretly hoped to hold the Heisman Trophy in ten years. Your children need to know that they are more than good enough.

They are yearning to hear from you that no matter what they do in life—good, bad, or indifferent—they are valid.

CHAPTER FIFTEEN
THE BASICS

I hope you know that I wrote this book because I'm looking out for your child's best interests.

It hurts my heart when a student comes in my door hungry in the morning. Please make sure your child is eating breakfast. For parents of teens, please don't let your child practice intermittent fasting, either.

According to FRAC, the Food Research and Action Center:

> Children and adolescents experiencing hunger have lower math scores and poorer grades.

> Students who skip breakfast are less able to differentiate among visual images, show increased errors, and have slower memory recall.

> Students who eat breakfast the morning of a standardized test have significantly higher scores in spelling, reading, and math, compared to those who do not eat breakfast.

> Children who eat breakfast show improved cognitive function, attention, and memory.

> Consuming breakfast improves children's performance on mathematical tasks, vocabulary tests, demanding mental tasks, and reaction to frustration.

You must make time in the morning to feed your children breakfast. Model healthy breakfast choices and routines by feeding yourself, too. If we want our children to develop healthy and sustainable habits, we also need to hold ourselves accountable. Beginning the day with breakfast is beyond essential to their development, cognition, and comprehension. Their academic aptitude depends so greatly on that initial sustenance in their stomachs before they arrive on campus.

You may think it silly, but I can literally tell the difference between a student who has had even the slightest bit of toast or cereal versus those who come in empty-stomached. It doesn't matter if you child tells you that they aren't hungry in the morning—don't buy it for a second. Core nuclear meltdowns are commonplace when tummies are empty and daily schedules are filled to the brim.

To assume that a child can learn and develop on an empty stomach, from eight in the morning until noon or even 12:30 p.m. when their lunch hour strikes, is ill-conceived. And we, as a community, are doing them a disservice by not insisting that they either walk out the door or into school with something to feed their minds and bodies. Peanut butter, toast, eggs, cereal . . . it doesn't have to be anything fancy or time-consuming to prepare. You can even embrace this as a teachable moment and instill self-reliance in your child by having them prepare something themselves. But no matter what—have them eat.

Many schools, in an effort to stem childhood hunger, offer free breakfast for students in the morning. This practice dates back to 1969 in Oakland, California, when the Black Panther Party sought to implement social change through a series of survival programs—free breakfast before school for hungry students was one of these. My school, like so many across the United States, has continued this tradition. We have cereal, string cheese, yogurt, and granola bars available for our students each morning. Some cafeterias have the capacity to offer hot meals. Is that something you could help advocate for or implement in your own school community?

They run and think and jump and play and problem solve and note-take and test-take and converse . . . all on zero fuel. That is a recipe for disaster.

Moving on—teachers and school staff are grateful for those of you who send your children to school with a fully stocked arsenal of pens, pencils, paper, and markers, and I salute you. But . . . do you ever replenish those? Ask yourself: Does the paper in the copy machine at my office stay stocked at all times? What about the coffee maker in the communal kitchen? Do your desk supplies of paper clips, notepads, and staples remain full? Do your dry erase markers ever run out; do you occasionally lose a pencil, or find you are one Post-it note short of a deck? Yep. The same thing happens to your child—only at a much higher rate. Take a look at the "must have" list I've compiled for you and your child to enable them to be prepared for whatever the year's curriculum throws their way, start to finish.

On top of the supplies that they house in their desks or tuck away in their backpacks, please send them with a free-reading book for when they have down-time in class. Encouraging a love of reading is crucial for your child's ongoing academic success, and it's never too late to pique their interest.

According to Jeffrey D. Wilhelm, professor of English education at Boise State University: "Data from major longitudinal studies show that pleasure reading in youth is the most explanatory factor of both cognitive progress and social mobility over time. . . . Pleasure reading is a more powerful predictor than even parental socioeconomic status and educational attainment."

Take time to browse your local bookstore, Amazon, or the *New York Times* bestseller list until something strikes their fancy. You can even use this as a vehicle for communication. It provides neutral ground, and can definitely give you an inlet into better understanding their thoughts, ideas, and feelings. And always, yes always, make sure that they have a lunch. Don't let your children's educational experience be jeopardized simply because they weren't prepared for what the day entailed.

BREAKFAST ITEMS

- peanut butter, almond butter, sunflower butter on whole grain toast
- whole grain cereal with milk
- banana or apple slices topped with a nut butter
- avocado toast
- yogurt with granola and fruit
- toaster waffle with nut butter
- scrambled eggs with whole grain toast
- fruit or greens smoothie
- a slice of turkey wrapped around a string cheese
- a hard boiled egg and a handful of berries
- oatmeal topped with apples, berries, nuts, etc.

SCHOOL SUPPLIES

GRADES K-2:

- crayons
- hand sanitizer
- colored folders
- #2 pencils
- eraser tops
- tissues
- spiral notebooks
- paper towels
- markers
- glue sticks
- pink erasers
- bandages

GRADES 3-5:

- plastic pencil box
- #2 pencils
- pink erasers
- red pens
- highlighters
- crayons
- fine-line washable markers
- wide-tip washable markers
- dry-erase markers, 4 count
- folders with pockets
- binders
- composition notebooks, college ruled
- binder paper, college ruled
- white liquid glue
- glue sticks
- school scissors
- 12-inch ruler (with inches and centimeters)
- clear tape
- protractor
- calculator
- paper towels
- tissues

CHAPTER SIXTEEN
I REPEAT, THE FOOTBALL WAS IN THE TOILET

It's recess, and I am just heading outside when I see a gaggle of boys clambering out of the bathroom and spilling out onto the play yard. They are rowdier than usual, which is saying a great deal, so their frenzy had me concerned.

Me: "What's the matter?"

Student #1: "Ew. Gross!"

Student #2: "Get it away from me!"

Me: "What's gross? Get what away from you? What's going on?"

Student #1: "The football was in the toilet."

Me: "The what?"

Student #2: "Yep—the football, *this football*, was in the toilet."

Me: (silence)

Boys: (uncontrollable laughter)

Cue the can of Lysol.

So, let me begin by answering a few initial questions: No, "football" was not some euphemism for what else is generally found in a toilet. In this case, the football was really in the toilet. At recess. In the boys' bathroom. And, you're right, these students would not let their playtime be deterred, so they went boldly where I certainly have never gone before—forearm deep in a public toilet to salvage their recess pick-up game's pigskin.

So many questions: Couldn't they have played basketball instead? Why didn't they ask for a pair of gloves? Did they wash their hands afterwards?

But, the question that stuck with me was—Why put a football in the toilet in the first place?

Having been in education now for fourteen-plus years, I have seen trends ebb and flow, strategies blow up and burn out, the rise of slime and the fall of frozen yogurt. And, while many things have left me feeling bewildered, one of the top contenders is just how little our kids appreciate things anymore.

The joy that once came from the simplicity of winning a Starburst after a math Bingo game has vanished. The thrill that used to permeate throughout the classroom at the very mention of a movie and popcorn prize is now dull. The excitement of a special art activity, an off-campus excursion, a new after-school club has been replaced by apathy.

And, the worst part of all? I think that it's far more disappointing for teachers than it is for our students.

I have said it to colleagues and friends alike—I often feel like I am fighting an unwinnable war. It's me (or, rather, teachers everywhere) against a culture of 24/7 instant gratification. Our kids subscribe to the notion of "I want it, I need it, and I have to have it—now!" Gone are the days of, over time, working to earn a prize, securing a reward, anticipating something special. We've arrived via warp speed at a place and time when nothing seems to be enough. Because, once they have what they asked for—like that football at recess—they are quick to dispose of it. Kick it over the fence, allow it to roll into the middle of oncoming traffic, dump it in the toilet. Where's the sanctity?

Case in point:

A colleague and friend of mine is an incredible art teacher. I mean, next-level talented. And, her lessons are the same. She brings to life the creative genius of her students through tactile projects, immersive field trips, and lots of choice (kids crave choice as they share the desire, much like us adults, to be in control).

But, I digress.

She and I were lamenting this very topic one evening over drinks. "Everything feels flat," she said. I agreed. She continued, "It's so frustrating, because I plan these exciting projects and activities, and it feels like the kids just don't care." From her vantage point, it doesn't matter if she brings out oil pastels, recyclable materials for a lifesize sculpture, or neon green acrylic—her students are no longer wowable.

Neither of us had a solution; it was more just a moment in time when we realized that the world has changed.

A culture and climate erected on the shaky foundation of all things disposable, the notion of permanence is lost on our kids. Taking time to craft something from scratch, harnessing patience, tenacity, and good ol' fashioned elbow grease is, more often than not, a thing of the past. Instead, our kids fumble and race from one activity to the next, failing to appreciate the here and now. They want to speed past whatever is in front of them to see what's next. And, God forbid whatever waits for them on the other side of the finish line isn't brighter and shinier than what they have currently. Well, then, you are left holding the proverbial bag—disappointed, dejected, and bummed out.

So, back to my football scenario. Why put it in the toilet?

Well . . . For starters, as I mentioned, not much seems to be sacred with our kids anymore. Sure, a few of my kids wanted so desperately to play football that they were willing to risk the hazmat exposure to get back their game piece, but in general, not much resonates. Language that used to be reserved for R-rated movies or fast-talking adults is now literally child's play, part of our kids' vernacular. Field trips are more of a chore to them than a reward, and if they aren't laced with a stop at 7-Eleven or free dress to sweeten the deal, then kids aren't interested. So sadly, it makes sense then, that a worn-out Nerf football wouldn't hold the same mystique today as it did in yesteryear.

Compound that with the idea that we live in a disposable society. Yes—we seek to be eco-conscious, recycling and composting when we can. But, when our brand new iPhones become obsolete before we even walk out of the store; when new Nike sneakers roll out faster than it takes to earn the money to purchase them; when I see lunches tossed out in their entirety and school supplies wasted and abandoned without the slightest concern, I realize that anything considered worn-in or worn-out, outdated or simply replaced by what's new and what's next, well, there is no way that a gently used and overly loved football would maintain its position as the apple of most kids' eyes today.

Splish splash.

Is there a solution? Can we change the course of this catastrophic mindset that we have somehow allowed to creep into child raising as we know it? Of course we can! But, it's going to take work, from each of us, from all of us, together.

Help your child understand the value of things: intrinsic, extrinsic, store-bought, and homemade. Place the same amount of importance on what's brand-spanking-new as you do with that which is a bit more worn. When you go shopping, give them a budget and have them understand how much things cost and the creative challenge that comes with living within one's means. Create a family pact to celebrate birthdays with at least one thing handmade (a card, a gift, breakfast-in-bed). Use chores and responsibilities as the baseline for earning privileges, so that they can develop an appreciation for the hard work it takes to one day make a living.

Teach your child skills: If a shirt loses a button, don't let them throw it out. Get out a needle and thread and show them how to sew it right back on. (Need guidance? YouTube has great lessons!). Show them how to polish scuffed shoes, mail in their worn out crayons to The Crayon Initiative (thecrayoninitiative.org), make pizzas together at home instead of ordering delivery. Each of these will help to develop within them an appreciation for what they have and what they need to do to maintain those things.

Talk to them: I realize that this seems very, very basic. But, without conversation, your child will not understand both your rationale or their part in the bigger picture. Discuss with them why you won't be upgrading their cell phone when the screen cracks; explain to them why they need to scrape their food scraps into the compost bin, turn the water off when they are brushing their teeth, drink from their reusable water bottle even if it is a bit dented. The more you communicate with your child, the more they will come to understand the whys of your guidance. They still may fight you on buying them the latest and greatest, but they will at least know that you have a reason for not.

Believe me, I get it—it's really hard to say "no" to your child. We all want to give them the world. But, we aren't doing them any favors by leading them to believe that the things given to them lack worth. That what they have currently can so easily fall short to what else is out there.

Let's team up, you and I, to get our kids excited again. And, in the process, let's keep footballs where they belong—on the playground, and out of the toilet.

CHAPTER SEVENTEEN

WOULD THE REAL EMILY POST PLEASE STAND UP?

Oh, puberty. We've all been there—the acne, the hair, the sweat, the smell. But the difference is—you have been there before, and your child has not. This is unchartered territory to them—scary at best. So if they are left to bungle and muddle their way through without any guidance from you, where does that leave them? They all will experience pimples or acne, so help them find solutions to ease their self-consciousness. Your daughters need to know about feminine hygiene products and how they are used. Don't let their periods be an exclamation point of shock and awe—prepare them for this change and let them know that they are OK. With the boys—teach them about shaving, showering, and remind them when it is time to get a haircut. Their fingernails should be trimmed and clean. Earwax has no place crawling outside of the ear. Greasy hair isn't a good look on anyone, so gently suggest that they wash it more frequently. I am not exaggerating here for effect—you really do need to have these discussions—repeatedly, I might add.

Let me invite you into my classroom of seventh graders on a rainy, humid day when all of the windows are closed, and the students have just returned from PE. It doesn't matter what age our children are; we, collectively, have a responsibility for their cleanliness. They could be three or thirteen—we must make sure that they understand the importance of fighting the proverbial funk.

Every year, it seems as though my students come to school dirtier, messier, and smellier than the last. Once-white shirts, dingy and stained; sweatshirts with holes and rips; mismatched socks and muddy shoes; fingernails with grime; hair with grease. . . . Do I need to describe the earwax and body odor?

I teach my students about hygiene because often their parents either haven't or don't. Believe me—I totally get the desire to avoid the uncomfortable! But this means that I then have to pull them aside and ask them if they use deodorant; did they happen to shower in the past three days; have they ever taken a brush to their nailbeds? These conversations are awkward at best.

But what's more awkward is if we sit by and allow them to become the victims of unkind comments or the butt of preteen jokes. Whether it was as a whole group or one-on-one with kiddos who displayed higher need than others, these were some of my strategies:

We talked about deodorant. What is it? Why do we need it? How do we use it and when? Where can we buy it, and how do we approach asking our parents to take us to the store to get some.

We talked about the necessity of frequent showering, especially after practice or an exceptionally rowdy recess. That as we grow older, our sweat begins to become the only thing that others can focus on when we are talking to them. And we want them to focus on the content of our communication instead.

I always kept a supply of pads and tampons in my classroom closet in case they needed one and were too nervous about asking the office staff for assistance.

A parent of one of my students owned a hotel and even brought in mini-bars of soap for each of the students to take home with them, aiming to help make hygiene accessible. Because the reality is that self-care is an added expense. And we need to find ways to make cleanliness an equitable reality for every student.

Have you talked to your kids about any of this? Have you taken them to the store and had them pick out a stick of deodorant? Have you set up a shower schedule to prevent funk and filth? I am not insinuating that you yourself are dirty, or that you run a house of horror. Far from it. What I am wondering, though, is whether you have these tough conversations with your child. Do you take the risk of the eye roll, the huff and puff, even the snarky remark back? Don't be afraid of uncomfortable moments. Talk to your child.

A friend of mine was recounting a story about how, after some time dating her now-husband, he began purchasing deodorant for her preteen daughter. When he would head out to the grocery store, the bag would come back with a new stick of deodorant, week after week. It got the point when the mother realized that he was gently nudging . . . moderately encouraging . . . alright, sending a very strong signal that something needed to change. Now, I totally understand that this was and would be a difficult conversation— the boyfriend telling his girlfriend's daughter that it was high time for some hygiene. Parents have to do more than imply to their kids. They will generally respond more fervently to candor over subtlety, so be blunt and frank with them.

"I love you, but we need to talk about body odor."

"I know it's cringey, but you and I need to have a conversation about taking more frequent showers."

"How about we head to the store and you can pick out a stick of deodorant to start using each day."

Don't humiliate them or make them feel small, just let them know that you are looking out for their own best interests, and you want to make sure that they are never put in an embarrassing situation with their peers. Your child should always know that you have their back.

We've morphed into Generation YouTube—a time and space where our students are relying upon the commentary of social media influencers for their know-how on everything from sex to hygiene to video game hacks. This is scary in that the online content available for their consumption is often not developmentally appropriate for their age or what they want to know. And when students are exposed to material that is beyond their comprehension, they begin to apply in real time terminology and behaviors that are wildly inappropriate, yet they can't quite grasp why these would be erroneous.

Big Mouth should not be how your child learns about the birds and the bees. Instagram shouldn't be where they discover how to shave or use a condom. These should be points of dialogue that come from you as parent, no matter how cringey the moment is when you begin this talk.

Chivalry has long ago been abandoned, and yet, if we hope to raise children of conviction and character, we will teach them the manners necessary for treating all people with respect. For example, we need to raise our kids to acknowledge all pronouns and celebrate all body types and physical abilities. But, we also need to ingrain in them second-nature considerations, like letting another classmate go ahead of them, whether it be walking into the building, standing in line for a drink of water, meandering down a crowded aisle in the chaos of the classroom. As an administrator, I have the great fortune of speaking with students of all ages about respect, empathy, and what it takes to be a good human. And, for our village to effectively cultivate good humans, we need to take time to address the concept of consent.

This dialogue can and should begin from the very beginning—when our kids are first learning to explore language and the ideas of sharing, taking turns, patience, and the boundaries of physical space. Asking for permission, in its many forms, doesn't stifle our children's independence or enslave them instead to dependency on the response of another. No. What it does do, however, is establish a permeating expectation of respect.

Even if you didn't talk with your kids when they were toddlers about consent, it's never too late—never! There are books to help illustrate this idea (a favorite of mine is *C Is for Consent*, by Eleanor Morrison), and there are a plethora of YouTube videos out there to guide you as well. Helping our children understand the necessity of asking another human's permission to give them a hug, a kiss, to hold their hand, or explore the boundaries of basic physical interaction is an imperative.

And, this is not just because of the light recently shone on the subject in the wake of the #metoo movement. Understanding consent helps your child, him- or her- or theirself, to feel empowered. To recognize that they have ownership over their own bodies, control to be able to say "no" when something feels uncomfortable, or that their voices, their opinions, their thoughts, ideas, and emotions are all valid. This is a necessity, and we—you and I—need to help our children understand its gravity.

Moving on—how do you approach conversations with your child on the topic of manners? Do they know to put their napkin in their lap, leave cell phones far away from the dinner table, push in their chairs when they get up from any room? These are basics. I have watched, horrified, as my students belch and burp their way through many an indoor lunch period. They are either too un-interested to care or they simply haven't been taught, but either way, it's a giant F—and we are failing them.

Eye contact, shaking hands when you meet someone new, holding the door open for others, saying "please" and "thank you" and "pardon me"—these should be absolutes and automatics, not exceptions. And I want you to know that if my colleagues and I are the only ones seeking to reinforce and reiterate these basic concepts of cordial human interactions, they will not stick. What happens then is that we are all left with a generation that lacks any sense of decorum.

Your child will not adopt these behaviors on a habitual basis because they are smart enough to know that when that bell rings at 3 p.m., they are out the door, off the hook, and can let it all hang out.

During the final song of a Soul Cycle class, the instructor told us a story. She recounted an experience where she taught several preteen girls alongside their moms. The girls had never taken the class before and required extra help from both the teacher and front desk staff members to get clipped in and ready to ride. During the final stretch, the girls talked and laughed, disrupting the calm of the studio. When class was over, the instructor said that all the girls walked right past her and out the door, without either saying "thank you" or acknowl-edging her.

It wasn't that she was seeking praise or compliments. "This isn't about me receiving any sort of personal gratification," she said. "The thing is, I don't blame the girls. No, I don't blame them at all. I blame their moms. I blame us, as a community. Because, together, we're not showing them the importance of saying 'thank you.'"

So when I teach students to push in their chairs when they leave their seats, I need to trust that you are modeling the same behavior at home. Likewise, I need you to reinforce respectful dialogue with your child, demanding of them that they do not talk back, exercise attitude, or use inappropriate language because I am confident that you are expecting the same of them when they get home.

And in the process of modeling better behavior—when we put our cell phones away for a moment, extend a gracious "gesundheit" to the stranger who sneezes, and take an extra moment to make eye contact with those whom we interact—we become better ourselves. And maybe this will make all of the difference.

CHAPTER EIGHTEEN
IT'S TIME TO LOG INTO LIFE

Our children have lost the ability to communicate.

"My kid is on her phone 24/7, texting and DMing friends."

That's what a mother told me about her teen. She was somber as she shared how being in her daughter's company, just chatting and talking about their days, was a distant memory, having morphed into a relationship that was divided by a screen between them. I hated to admit how right she was, for it is a sad reality that teachers have recognized for years. Only now, the realization is seeping its way out of the classroom and into the minds and hearts of saddened observers. We just aren't talking anymore.

That's because texting and instant messaging is not communication. Communicating genuinely means you are sitting across from or next to someone and engaging in an actual dialogue. You are asking questions, listening, and making eye contact.

In both adults and youth, it's rare to see people making eye contact, giving firm handshakes, listening and responding appropriately, asking follow-up questions relevant to the topic at hand. I want more than anything to bring this back.

It breaks my heart, both as an English teacher and as one who loves a good conversation, that for our children, any dialogue lacking in emojis or abbreviations has become a foreign concept. It's as if they aren't even talking if they're not using eggplants and winky faces and cartoon poop.

I became an English teacher because I desperately wanted to help my students, the next generation, fall head over heels in love with the written word, as I have. And I do believe that I accomplished that on many levels. Can my classroom microcosm alter the trajectory of where human communication is headed? On its own? Certainly not. But if we begin to work together, collectively holding kids accountable for what they say and how they say it? Then, absolutely.

Every year, in my eighth-grade class, I was on a mission to teach my students the nuances of successful interviewing. They weren't quite ready to join the workforce, but they did need to prepare for high school interviews with admissions counselors. Even students who were choosing to attend public schools that do not require admission rituals could and did still benefit from this lesson. Why? Because the art of conversation has been lost.

I wish that I had just one example. One moment that stands out above the rest when I watched a student approach their parent or guardian with exciting news, something really important to tell them, or just in need of an embrace, and instead of giving them their 100 percent, undivided attention, their parents' eyes were instead diverted to the screen of their device.

The time when one of my seventh-grade students had finally achieved an A minus on their essay, and as they went out to show it to their mom, she put up one finger to have her child "hang on" while she continued to type her text.

The fifth-grade student who came bounding out of the school doors, arms wide open to give his mom a hug when she was picking him up early, and she walked right past him to the car while talking to someone else on her smartphone.

Ask yourself this question: *How many times have I been "talking" with someone all the while scrolling through emails, sports scores, or text messages on my phone? How many times do I ask that person to repeat the question or feign a generic response hoping that they won't notice my lack of engagement?* Own it—we all have done this. The problem is that we have the interpersonal skills to barely—*barely*—bridge the gap. Our children, however, do not. So instead of scrambling to appear the slightest bit engaged, they simply tune out the conversation altogether. Partly due to the fact that they are of the age when their self-absorption is at its peak, and partly because they haven't been taught the ins and outs of being present in the moment. How can we blame them when we fall victim to the same habit?

Cell phones on the dinner table, the diminishment of family meals altogether, and the prevalence of text messaging as our primary mode of communication are making our children unable to engage socially.

You, as the parent, can make sure your child doesn't feel lost after high school graduation. You have the power to alter this collision course of communication calamities. Insist on conversing with your child. Draw them into dialogue and discussion with you.

Ask questions that might be on the cusp of probing, yet not quite so invasive.

"Tell me about something that went really well for you today."

"I've been getting the impression that you've been feeling anxious. How can I help?"

"This has seemed like an intense week for both of us. Why don't you tell me about yours first."

"How did that science test go that we studied for together last night?

What was the essay question about?"

"You haven't mentioned your friend James in awhile. Everything OK?"

It is a fine line, but with practice, you will come to realize that not only will your understanding and appreciation of your son or daughter blossom, but their ability to answer questions with candor and authenticity will grow in the process.

One of my best friends has been bringing her son out to dinner with her and her husband since infancy. It's one of the things that I admire about her—she believed in assimilating him into social situations from the get-go.

You know what else is truly amazing about her? She doesn't allow him to be on a tablet or a device throughout the entire duration of the evening. He is there, present in conversation, even if it's well beyond his years of comprehension. He is engaged, he is listening, and one day, he'll have the social graces to look another diner in the eye and either agree wholeheartedly with what they are saying, or have the evolved courage to verbalize his own counterpoints. Either way—she has raised him to see the world without a screen blocking his full immersion into life.

The next step is the hardest one, but it has to, has to be done. Ready? You have to limit your kids' time on technology. *Gulp!* I know, it sounds like a unicorn— completely and totally unfathomable. But it is essential. Not just for them. But for yourself, too. You have to be willing to model that life doesn't stop when we unplug; when we put our phones on Do Not Disturb; when we go for a walk and leave our devices behind. We will survive, and our kids will, in turn, thrive.

Author Meredith Hale recounted her own experience in the *Washington Post:*

> I had become an addict.
>
> I was addicted to my iPhone.
>
> It started innocently enough. I would check email throughout the day, mostly for work. Soon I found myself checking Facebook first thing in the morning, and sneaking peeks at my blog before going to bed. Eventually I reached the point where I'd even check my weather app for a fix.

Technology addiction is a real thing. Hale is not alone. We are all guilty at one time or another of putting our devices ahead of interpersonal interactions. It's not just the devices themselves that are creating a tether for users—apps and games can be just as enslaving. A recent article in the *New York Times* about social media video app TikTok reported that: "TikTok's addictiveness can be traced, in part, to its use of artificial intelligence to anticipate what users want and fill their feeds with it. That technology is so effective that the app's owner, Bytedance (a Chinese conglomerate), last year introduced anti-addiction measures in Douyin, the Chinese version, to help both users and the parents who may be worried about them."

Not only does technology create tension between kids and their parents—and their teachers!—studies done by Common Sense Media show that technology use may be related to lower empathy and social well-being. "Many researchers have noted that narcissism seems to be increasing, while empathic traits have been on the decline, and have pointed to social media as a driver for that change. . . . Time spent with media could subtract from face-to-face time, so heavy media users would forfeit opportunities to deepen empathy by conversing and learning from human facial and vocal cues."

I am definitely not telling you to take it away altogether or even for an egregious amount of time. Just a little. Maybe it's when they first get home from school. You could even go so far as to use it as bait—"After we have a chance to catch up on our days and talk about what's been going on, then you'll get it right back." Maybe you're making dinner, and you let your child watch a show after setting the table.

This doesn't have to be as bad or as painful as it sounds—the two of you, sitting at the kitchen table, the wall clock tick-tick-ticking in the background as you stare at each other in awkward silence. No. Conversation can be over tactile experiences—flipping through a magazine, making a snack together, or doing the dishes. Eventually you'll want to move into exercises in eye contact and such. But for now, just start small. Baby steps. No cell phone or tablet for a few minutes. Just talk.

In addition to enhancing your relationship with your child, it is also a way that we can partner together, you and I, teacher and parent. Most schools either do not allow or severely limit the use of cell phones in class.

The teachers at my school collect cell phones and smart watches at the start of each day, returning them only when students head home. We have a classroom box for all students in grades three through eight. At the start of the morning, a designated student in each classroom collects all of the students' devices and brings the box downstairs to the office, where it is kept safe until the end of the day. If a parent or guardian needs to reach their child, they call the office, and we relay the message. The students' attention and focus need to be on learning and engaging and taking part in every aspect of the academic process.

CONVERSATION CAN
BE OVER TACTILE
EXPERIENCES—FLIPPING
THROUGH A MAGAZINE,
MAKING A SNACK
TOGETHER, OR DOING
THE DISHES.

First and foremost, phones and smart watches are a distraction. The more that I collect these devices and house them in my office, the more I realize how tethered our students are to them. They buzz and chirp and ping literally every two minutes—maybe not a text each time, but a news alert, a Snapchat notification, a message from a fellow gamer. Students have become enslaved to the constant bombardment of outside influences that, when they are in a learning environment, decrease their capacity for academic immersion.

Additionally, time spent staring at a screen impacts the way students read and absorb information, limiting their capacity for reading comprehension, an essential skill set for success. Engage your kids with the physical world of books— ink, paper, weight in their hands, and texture on their fingertips. As noted in the *New Yorker*, "Being a Better Online Reader":

> The online world . . . tends to exhaust our resources more quickly than the page. . . . Our eyes themselves may grow fatigued from the constantly shifting screens, layouts, colors, and contrasts, an effect that holds for e-readers as well as computers. Mary Dyson, a psychologist at the University of Reading . . . has found that the layout of a text can have a significant effect on the reading experience. We read more quickly when lines are longer, but only to a point. When lines are too long, it becomes taxing to move your eyes from the end of one to the start of the next. . . . Online, you can find yourself transitioning to entirely new layouts from moment to moment, and, each time you do so, your eyes and your reading approach need to adjust. Each adjustment, in turn, takes mental and physical energy.

> Beyond all of this, smartphones and devices can be and are used to assist in cheating.

Answers to every test question, prewritten essays, summaries of novels taught, shortcuts to online learning platforms—when students are able to peruse the Internet without regulation or supervision, original thought and their capacity to create are paralyzed.

Any student caught with a device outside of collection time is required to remand it to my care in the front office until the day's end, sometimes longer if they are a repeat offender.

I have had students come to my office, "just to check on" their phones. They feel compelled to hold them for just a moment or two, probe me for info about whether anyone has texted them, called them, can they check their IG stories?

"No, you cannot," is how I start my response.

I go on to reiterate that they should be focusing on the tangible in these moments—the sound of their teacher's voice as they impart knowledge to them in a math lesson. The glimmer in the eye of a classmate who has successfully landed a well-crafted joke. The smell of hot lunch in the cafeteria, the feeling of holding an A+ paper, or the vibrating impact of giving a teammate a high five during PE. These are the experiences that should be occupying their time, thoughts, and energy—not what they are missing out on in the vacuous digital world.

At our school dances, part of the attendance agreement is that there are no phones allowed in the gym. "But how am I going to enjoy the dance without it?" one student asked me.

"I want you to live life without the filter of a screen in front of you," I replied. "I want you to make memories with your mind. Photographic evidence that you were at the dance doesn't make it any more valid of an experience," I told them. They weren't thrilled with my response, but their feedback on Monday morning as how great the dance was, was all the validation I needed.

While I am stressing the message to my students that they have only this moment, this day, this class, to seize the opportunity at hand, I need to know that you, as a parent, are echoing that same message at day's end. When you are engaging with your children without screens, you are giving them the greatest gift—the present of the present.

A 2016 census conducted by Common Sense Media on technology use by both parents and their children revealed that:

> Fifty percent of parents indicated that they thought using social media hurts children's physical activity.
>
> Parents are "moderately" or "extremely" worried about kids spending too much time online (43 percent), oversharing personal details (38 percent), accessing online pornography (36 percent), and being exposed to images or videos of violence (36 percent).
>
> Two-thirds (67 percent) of parents said that monitoring child media use is more important than respecting their children's privacy.
>
> A majority of parents report that mobile devices are not allowed during family meals (78 percent) or bedtime (63 percent).

One more thing . . . you have to take the challenge, too. I know and appreciate how busy you are—I really do. But you are the greatest teacher and model your child has. According to Common Sense Media's founder and CEO James P. Steyer: "Media can add a lot of value to relationships, education, and development, and parents clearly see the benefits, but if they are concerned about too much media in their kids' lives, it might be time to reassess their own behavior so that they can truly set the example they want for their kids."

If you commit to reigniting the art of conversation in your home, it will be much easier for your child to emulate. Children hate hypocrisy. So let them see you're on the same team, playing by the same rules. And from there, all you have to do is just enjoy the game.

CHAPTER NINETEEN
BURST THE BUBBLE

Seeing how disconnected our kids are today hurts my heart. After school, instead of watching kids chat and laugh with one another, they're plugged into their devices. The second they retrieve them from their classroom's box at the end of the day, their eyes are immediately glued to their screens again, getting the digital fix they have craved all day.

It hasn't always been like this. When I first started teaching, sure, students had cell phones. But when school let out, they would grab a basketball and shoot hoops while waiting to be picked up. They would sit in a circle and talk—about the day's events, about what they were going watch on TV, about me. It doesn't matter now what the content of the conversation was—it matters that they were *talking*. They were connecting on a human-to-human level.

Every year, I would take my students to volunteer with a San Francisco-based organization to feed lunch to the city's homeless men and women. GLIDE Foundation provides numerous opportunities for adults, children, even families to serve 2,000 meals a day in San Francisco's Tenderloin neighborhood. Even though some of them had previously completed other service learning projects, they witnessed an unparalleled level of destitution at this particular shelter. I always signed my students up to work in both the kitchen and dining room, adding food to trays, pouring water, bussing tables, and greeting each guest as they arrived. The lessons in gratitude with which they walked away were astounding.

"I was complaining to my mom this morning about how I didn't like what she made for breakfast. These people don't have breakfast."

"There was one guy in there who didn't have any shoes. I've never seen that before, like, in real life."

"I need to tell my mom 'thank you' for sending me to school so that I don't end up there."

"I was scared about going. But I want to do that again."

It's far too easy to write a check; to drop a few quarters into the plastic cup of a street beggar is too neat. This is why we need to get kids out of their bubbles, their routines, the perfection of their schedules. Volunteer at a homeless shelter and serve lunch to its residents to develop an appreciation in your child for the stability of consistent shelter and meals. Embark on various modes of transportation to get to and from school, helping your child exercise their self-reliance to navigate their way home. Expose them to the foods and traditions of their own heritage as well as the cultures of their friends and community. And push their comfort zone by challenging them to go without, to be resourceful with what they have versus focusing on what they don't.

Make an effort to model to your child the behavior you would like to see in them. This is a blanket statement that can be applied to many areas of your child's development, but for now, let's just focus on generosity and thoughtfulness. In order for your child to believe that taking care of others is a priority, you must build that into your own daily routine. When it comes time to shop for Christmas gifts, talk to your child about what their teacher, coach, or friend likes, or engage them in a game where they play "I spy" to see what any of these individuals need. Build within your child an awareness of others and a perception of what those people require.

One year, I for some reason was always looking for sticky notes. I would search high and low, eventually scamming them from one of my students. Now who was the one unprepared for class?

That Christmas, I received a gift wrapped in far too much snowman paper with a prefab bow affixed to the top among a crowd of Scotch tape. A card was there too, with a simple message: "Now you won't have borrow ours." It was a six-pack of Post-it notes. And while the gesture may have come from sheer annoyance at my begging, it was one of the most thoughtful gifts I have ever received as a teacher; my student took the time to select a gift that meant something to me. It let me feel that while I was busy taking care of that class of thirty-something preteens, one of them was taking care of me. Never has paper meant so much.

A number of my friends have begun to have babies of their own, and one girlfriend in particular, who's a teacher, deserves a big gold star. She has been a driving force of inspiration for much of this book not only because we talked over the years, as colleagues, about our hopes for our students and our despair at parenting trends we found distressing, but because even when she began having children of her own, she never relinquished those pillars which we know to be essential.

I find the way she is raising her sons worthy of applause. For example, she has decided that they will not be chained to a schedule. That they will go with her and her husband out to dinner, join in on spontaneous road trips, and not worry if the tailgate before a Stanford University football game interferes with their naptime routine. She recognizes, of course, the need for rest for her sons, and she certainly gives them downtime in the day to sleep. But she also knows that immersing them in a world of flexibility, one that ebbs and flows with the unpredictable, gives them the skills to adapt when changes occur throughout their lives.

Notice that I use the word *chained*. That is because, while both she and I understand the essentiality of boundaries, rules, parameters, and routine for children and adolescents, we also know that too much of anything leads to negative consequences—wine, fried foods, television, and yes, even schedules. If your child is so trained to react and respond on cue, they lack the ability to function when the slightest curveball is thrown their way. Teachers everywhere have seen it—when all of a sudden, PE class has been moved to later in the afternoon, or a Chromebook's battery dies without warning, or basketball practice has been cancelled altogether—alarm bells sound as overprogrammed kiddos spin into a whirlwind of anxiety and stress.

Another friend has taken her children around the world. At just two and three years of age, they had long ago been brought into the fold of their parents' love for backpacking and sightseeing and experiencing the vastness of what's out there to explore. My friend knows how to nurse in the middle of a parking garage while buckling her other child into their car seat. Knows how to pack for four in carry-on luggage that includes ten days' worth of diapers. Knows that playing baseball games in the living room and watching hockey games on a Tuesday night will create indelible memories and a spirit of flexibility in her children. My friend knows the richness of child development that comes from allowing her kids to live free range—a childhood of inquiry and discovery.

I was having coffee with a former student, and as we were discussing her experiences in high school, her future plans for college and beyond, I asked her how she was feeling about the future.

"Looking back at high school, how did you feel about it?" I asked. "And how are you feeling about what's next?"

Her response was pragmatic, but direct. "I feel really good about how I did in high school," she said, "But I'm anxious about the future." She was afraid to leave its bubble.

She's not alone. So many kids grow up with a strict routine that leaves little room for variety and diversity socioeconomically, culturally, experientially. She described yearning to interact with a far broader spectrum of individuals—those who hadn't walked the same path she has. The majority of students with whom she was interacting seemed to come from the same backgrounds—successful, college-educated parents, solid incomes, expensive cars. "I realize that the rest of the world isn't like that. How will I know how to relate to kids who don't have it all?"

How are you opening your kid's eyes to new experiences, other cultures, and people they might not meet in their daily lives? How are you increasing the scope of their knowledge and awareness? It doesn't mean that you have to break the bank by taking them on exotic vacations to the far corners of the earth.

Here are some ways you might get your kids get out of their bubbles and learn about the realities of others:

> Write letters to soldiers abroad and study the demographics of where they're stationed.

> Put together care packages for people serving time and talk about criminal justice.

> Collaborate with your son or daughter's school to organize a jacket or book drive for your community and ask older students to distribute these items to men and women living on the street.

This brings me to another noticeable trend in education: how many young adults feel the pressure to stay on one path, the path to college right after high school. We have become so focused on insisting that every student enters college at age eighteen that we no longer provide the opportunity to develop other talents, interests, and the tools necessary to live independently.

Yes, I believe that every young person deserves the chance to go to college. But I also believe that if you take another route—by, say, learning a trade—you can find your way.

Let me explain. Back in the day, high school coursework included the basics of reading, writing, math, and science. But beyond that, students learned home economics, auto shop, even carpentry. Perhaps these students still pursued a career in marketing or accounting, but they also learned trade skills upon which they could both rely and fall back if necessary.

One of my friends is a highly acclaimed makeup artist who was raised in Russia by her mother, a home ec teacher. Over dinner, she told a story of a time when she was doing the makeup of a high-profile celebrity for a red carpet event when the starlet's vintage dress ripped a small hole in the back. There was panic over what would be the eventual outcome of the tear and what backup outfits were available at the last minute. But my friend said, "I can sew that for you." Because she had been taught the basics of seam-stressing as a child, she was able to put those skills to work in a pinch. Crisis averted; red carpet saved.

It doesn't matter if it's teaching the technique to hard boil an egg, balance a bank account, build credit, fix a missing button, or use a screwdriver. In the end, I believe we need to teach every kid how to be self-reliant.

CONCLUSION
THE END IS ONLY THE BEGINNING

No one told me when I signed up to be a teacher that this would be easy. The minutes and hours in the classroom have been challenging. Likewise, when that proverbial pee stick announced you were going to be a parent, or when that ultrasound confirmed there was a little new and magnificent being on the way, there was still no guarantee this would be easy.

Teachers enter the classroom because we love to nurture children. We aim to be kind and humble, and when you are concerned, most likely we are, too. When you are elated, share that joy with your kids' teachers. Let them feel the same enthusiasm you do. When you both can't seem to come to an agreement on an issue, take a time-out. Decide upon an agreeable time to reconvene, and use the moments in between to contemplate what was proposed by the opposing side.

You have been given the greatest opportunity in the world as a parent. I wrote this book because I want you to know that you are not alone. You have a network of support at school, including teachers who are there to encourage you, and administrators who want the exact same thing that you do—for your child to succeed.

A friend of mine said it best: "As a parent, you are not just raising a child—you are raising a human being."

So together, let's raise the best human beings we can.

NOTES:

REFERENCES

BOOKS:

Bailey, Jacqui. *Sex, Puberty, and All That Stuff.* (Hauppauge, NY: B. E. S. Publishing, 2004)

Gravelle, Karen. *The Period Book: Everything You Don't Want to Ask (But Need to Know).* (London: Piatkus Books, 1997)

Madaras, Lynda, Area Madaras, and Simon Sullivan. *What's Happening to My Body? Book for Boys.* (New York: HarperCollins Publishers, 2009)

Mayle, Peter. *What's Happening to Me? An Illustrated Guide to Puberty.* (Fort Lee, NJ: Lyle Stuart, 2000)

Natterson, Cara. *The Care and Keeping of You 2.* (Middleton, WI: American Girl, 2013)

Nuchi, Adah. *Bunk 9's Guide to Growing Up.* (New York: Workman, 2017)

Schaefer, Valorie. *The Care and Keeping of You.* (Middleton, WI: American Girl, 2012)

WEBSITES:

Crisis Text Line: https://www.crisistextline.org/

National Parent Helpline: https://www.nationalparenthelpline.org/

No Bully: https://www.nobully.org/

Stopbullying.gov. https://www.stopbullying.gov/

Young Minds Advocacy: https://www.ymadvocacy.org/

ONLINE SOURCES:

Coldridge, Alison (writer). "Nicole Richie On Parenting: 'Kids Want to Be Told The Truth.'" Mother & Baby. https://www.motherandbaby.co.uk/lifestyle-and-celebs/celebrity-mums/nicole-richie-on-parenting-kids-want-to-be-told-the-truth

Common Sense Media. Children, Teens, Media, and Body Image Info-graphic. January 20, 2015. https://www.commonsensemedia.org/children-teens-body-image-media-infographic

Common Sense Media. "How is body image affected by social media and going online?" https://www.commonsensemedia.org/media-and-body-image/how-is-body-image-affected-by-social-media-and-going-online

Common Sense Media. "New Report: Parents Spend More Than Nine Hours a Day with Screen Media." December 6, 2016. https://www.commonsensemedia.org/about-us/news/press-releases/new-report-parents-spend-more-than-nine-hours-a-day-with-screen-media

Common Sense Media. "Technology Addiction: Concern, Controversy, and Finding Balance." Research brief (PDF), 2016. https://www.commonsensemedia.org/sites/default/files/uploads/research/csm_2016_technology_addiction_research_brief_0.pdf

Elgersma, Christine. "The Facts about Online Predators Every Parent Should Know." Common Sense Media, July 25, 2017. https://www.commonsensemedia.org/blog/the-facts-about-online-predators-every-parent-should-know

Food Research and Action Center (FRAC). "Breakfast for Learning." https://frac.org/research/resource-library/breakfast-for-learning

Hale, Meredith. "My iPhone addiction was making me a terrible mom." *The Washington Post*, March 9, 2015. https://www.washingtonpost.com/news/parenting/wp/2015/03/09/my-iphone-addiction-was-making-me-a-terrible-mom/

Haller, Sonja. "Meet the 'lawnmower parent,' the new helicopter parents of 2018." *USA Today*, September 19, 2018; updated September 20, 2018. https://www.google.com/amp/s/amp.usatoday.com/amp/1347358002

Hinkelman, Lisa. "The Girls' Index: New insights into the complex world of today's girls." Ruling Our eXperiences, 2017. https://static1.squarespace.com/static/597249b6d7bdcec54c7fdd10/t/59cec40132601ed-2cee562bd/1506722842794/Girls%27+Index+Research+Brief+Final.pdf

Horne, Corrina. "What Is Adolescent Egocentrism, And How Can I Deal With It As A Parent?" Betterhelp, January 30, 2020. https://www.betterhelp.com/advice/adolescence/what-is-adolescent-egocentrism-and-how-can-i-deal-with-it-as-a-parent/

Komisar, Erica. "Don't Believe in God? Lie to Your Children." *Wall Street Journal*, December 5, 2019. https://www.wsj.com/articles/dont-believe-in-god-lie-to-your-children-11575591658

Konnikova, Maria. "Being a Better Online Reader." *The New Yorker*, July 16, 2014. https://www.newyorker.com/science/maria-konnikova/being-a-better-online-reader

Lorenz, Taylor. "High Schools to TikToK: We're Catching Feelings." *The New York Times*, October 19, 2019; updated October 20, 2019. https://www.nytimes.com/2019/10/19/style/high-school-tiktok-clubs.html

Malik Chua, Jasmin. "The environment and economy are paying the price for fast fashion—but there's hope." Vox, Sep 12, 2019. https://www.vox.com/2019/9/12/20860620/fast-fashion-zara-hm-forever-21-boohoo-environment-cost

National Alliance on Mental Illness. "Teens & Young Adults." https://www.nami.org/find-support/teens-and-young-adults

National Institute of Mental Health (NIMH). "Child and Adolescent Mental Health." May 2019. https://www.nimh.nih.gov/health/topics/child-and-adolescent-mental-health/index.shtml

National Runaway Safeline. "How to protect against bullying." https://www.1800runaway.org/2017/10/resources-for-bullying-victims/

Pearson, Catherine. "The Benefits Of Writing With Good Old Fashioned Pen And Paper." Huffpost, September 12, 2014; updated December 6, 2017. https://www.huffpost.com/entry/writing-on-paper_n_5797506

Staff. "How writing by hand makes kids smarter." *The Week*, October 6, 2010. https://theweek.com/articles/490493/how-writing-by-hand-makes-kids-smarter

Wilhelm, Jeffrey D. "The Benefits of Reading for Pleasure." Edutopia, October 30, 2017. https://www.edutopia.org/article/benefits-reading-pleasure